Elizabeth I
CEO

⊰ABOUT THE AUTHOR⊱

Alan Axelrod is the author of the national *Business Week* bestseller *Patton on Leadership: Strategic Lessons for Corporate Warfare*, based on the philosophy and battlefield victories of General George S. Patton, and of the national bestseller *What Every American Should Know About American History: 200 Events That Shaped the Nation*. His many other works of military history, military biography, and general history include *Dictators and Tyrants*; *The War Between the Spies: A History of Espionage During the American Civil War*; *Chronicle of the Indian Wars: From Colonial Times to Wounded Knee*; *Complete Idiot's Guide to American History*; and *Encyclopedia of the American West*. He has also written numerous books on management, business communications, and career development.

Axelrod studied history and English at Northeastern Illinois University, and went on to receive his Ph.D. in English, with an emphasis on American literature and civilization, from the University of Iowa. He taught at several colleges before embarking on a career in publishing. After holding executive positions at the Henry Francis Du Pont Winterthur Museum, Van Nostrand Reinhold, and Abbeville Press, he became Director of Development for Turner Publishing, Inc., a subsidiary of Turner Broadcasting System, based in Atlanta. Since 1997, he has been President of The Ian Samuel Group, Inc., a book packaging and consulting firm. He specializes in bringing together authors and publishing professionals with hands-on experience in a variety of fields to create major works of reference for professional and general audiences.

Elizabeth I
CEO

STRATEGIC LESSONS FROM
THE LEADER
WHO BUILT AN EMPIRE

ALAN AXELROD

Prentice
Hall Press

Library of Congress Cataloging-in-Publication Data

Axelrod, Alan.
    Elizabeth I, CEO : strategic lessons from the leader who built an empire. /
Alan Axelrod.
        p.   cm.
    Includes bibliographical references (p.) and index.
    ISBN 0-7352-0189-7 — ISBN 0-7352-0357-1 (pbk.)
    1. Elizabeth I, Queen of England, 1533-1603—Views on leadership.
2. Queens—Great Britain—Biography.   3. Leadership.   I. Title.
DA355.A94 2000
942.05'5'092—dc21   00-034691
                                                                            CIP

Acquisitions Editor: *Tom Power*
Production Editor: *Sharon L. Gonzalez*
Formatter: *Robyn Beckerman*
Designer: *Tom Nery*

Printed in the United States of America

10 9 8 7 6 5 4 3 2 1

ISBN 0-7352-0357-1

ATTENTION: CORPORATIONS AND SCHOOLS

Prentice Hall books are available at quantity discounts with bulk purchase for
educational, business, or sales promotional use. For information, please write
to: Prentice Hall Special Sales, 240 Frisch Court, Paramus, New Jersey 07652.
Please supply: title of book, ISBN, quantity, how the book will be used, date
needed.

 Paramus, NJ 07652

http://www.phdirect.com

For Anita, my queen

⊰TABLE OF CONTENTS⊱

❧INTRODUCTION❧

The last year of the old century, 1999, witnessed the usual Hollywood harvest of movies, most bulging with the requisite stock of car chases, explosions, dismemberments, supernatural horrors, sexual misalliances, and bathroom humor. Among these, however, was one highly unlikely blockbuster, *Elizabeth*, the film biography of a 466-year-old queen of England. Literate, rich in subtlety, immersing the viewer in a remote and highly complex time, *Elizabeth* was hard to imagine as a big box-office draw. But, then, who could have imagined, 466 years earlier, that a slender, pale, golden-red-haired girl, frail in health, declared a bastard by her ruthless father and an uncompromising Parliament, held prisoner through much of her childhood, under a cloud of accusation of treason, would survive to adulthood, let alone assume, at age twenty-five, the throne of England?

And not just *survive* to become queen, but to become the greatest monarch ever to rule England, a leader who bequeathed her name to a golden age of English achievement and culture—

indeed, a consummate example of effective leadership that has endured for five centuries and will doubtless endure for many more.

So Elizabeth I is a fascinating woman, a great monarch, and a figure of extraordinary historical importance. You, on the other hand, are a supervisor, a manager, an executive, a CEO, a boss. Your business isn't a royal realm, and your staff is certainly not your lowly and beholden subjects. What, then, can you learn from this woman who took her nation from the bottom of the European barrel to the summit of the world's great powers?

You can learn that being a leader is being a leader, whether your enterprise is a renaissance kingdom, a small business, a major corporation, a corporate department, or a three-person work group with a job to do. *Elizabeth I, CEO* distills and delivers the key leadership lessons of a long, challenging, and highly successful reign, a leadership career that turned a failing enterprise around and shaped the enduring destiny of a people.

"An Elizabethan Prologue" fills you in on the dysfunctional family and barely functioning world from which Elizabeth came and also furnishes an executive summary of the queen's career. The ten chapters that follow the prologue explore that career in selective detail, drawing from it concise lessons for leadership in ten key leadership areas:

1. A leader's first lesson: survival
2. Creating a leadership image

3. Combining the common touch with the air of leadership

4. Creating common cause without tyranny

5. Building a loyal staff—and a loyal opposition

6. Growing the enterprise and crushing the competition

7. Turning crisis into triumph

8. Holding on to the power

9. Doing business without excuses

10. Winning—and what it means

Before you read on, ponder this statement of unadorned fact: When Elizabeth was crowned in 1558, England was a victim of itself and of its competitors, almost too far behind them even to be called an also-ran. When Elizabeth died in 1603, having reigned for forty-five years, England was the richest and most powerful nation in Europe and well on its way to becoming the greatest empire the world would ever know.

How did she turn her organization around?

This is both the underlying and overarching question *Elizabeth I, CEO* endeavors to answer in each chapter and each episode drawn from the queen's life and reign.

Now, just what can *you* learn from the turnaround *she* achieved?

That depends on who "you" are. The great Victorian philosopher-historian Thomas Carlyle declared that history is neither more nor less than the biography of great men (today, he would have said great men and women), and the American philosopher George Santayana famously pronounced that those who fail to learn the lessons of history are doomed to repeat the errors of the past. Few lives are filled with more historical significance than that of Elizabeth; few lives have as many lessons to teach. *Anyone* who reads and heeds the life of Elizabeth may come away from the experience enriched. But this book is not directed at just *anyone*. It is aimed specifically at the leaders of today, the builders and would-be builders of contemporary empires. It is directed at top executives as well as middle managers and those just embarking on their careers. The life of Elizabeth has much to say to those beginning their climb up the corporate ladder as well those who, having attained the top rung, do not want to slip from it. The queen's long reign offers lessons on how to

- develop a leadership attitude
- develop leadership skills
- develop a leadership image
- develop and exhibit personal dynamism
- communicate effectively
- establish priorities
- set objectives and goals
- inspire others
- manipulate others ethically
- create loyalty
- build a team
- resolve conflict effectively

- be an effective coach and mentor
- lead by example while minimizing micromanagement
- nurture creative thought in others
- know the "enemy" (your competition)
- create outstanding production
- create maximum performance
- create exceptional quality

Most of all, the career of Elizabeth I is an example of vision, of creating vision, of communicating vision, and of realizing vision.

Who will learn the most from *Elizabeth I, CEO*? Those men and women who want to grow their enterprise, grow their career, grow their company, and who can already dream and are ready now to build what they dream.

Elizabeth both led and managed England as a brilliant executive runs a great corporation, treating it as a dynamic system based perhaps on certain unchanging, transcendent principles, but always responsive to the circumstances of a fluid world. Her five-centuries-old saga is also very much a story of today and a story you can use. Just bear in mind that there is "some assembly required." Mining the past for the nuggets that still shine brightly requires limbering your historical imagination, especially when half a millennium separates us from the original events. I invite you, then, to begin this book at the beginning. The prologue is intended to make all that follows most immediately and fully relevant to you and your needs.

"The burden that has fallen upon me maketh me amazed."

—ELIZABETH,
three days after becoming queen of England

AN ELIZABETHAN
PROLOGUE

WILLIAM SHAKESPEARE, CERTAINLY THE GREATEST playwright to live under the reign of Elizabeth, described England this way in *King Richard II*:

> *This royal throne of kings, this scepter'd isle,*
> *This earth of majesty, this seat of Mars,*
> *This other Eden, demi-paradise . . .*
> *This blessed plot, this earth, this realm, this England . . .*

The Bard wrote these words about 1595, the thirty-seventh year of Elizabeth's reign. Some four decades earlier, England made a considerably less positive impression on an anonymous traveler. "The arse of the world," he called it. More generally and more delicately in those years immediately preceding Elizabeth's ascension to the throne, the island kingdom was routinely referred to as "this unhappy realm."

1

"THIS UNHAPPY REALM"

When Elizabeth ascended the throne in 1558, one of her subjects summed up the sorry state of the nation:

> *England lay now most afflicted, embroiled on the one side with the Scottish, on the other side with the French war; overcharged with debt . . . the treasury exhausted; Calais . . . lost, to the great dishonour of the English nation; the people distracted with different opinions in religion; the Queen bare of potent friends, and strengthened with no alliance of foreign princes.*

England in 1558 was an economic and cultural backwater, impoverished, burdened by runaway inflation, cursed with a debased currency, possessing neither an army nor a navy to speak of, torn internally by religious dissension propelling the country toward civil war, faced with enemies in Scotland (at the time a foreign country), plagued by rebellion in Ireland (only nominally an English realm), eyed greedily by the French, the Spanish, and the Holy Roman Empire, its pitiful throne contested by more than a few pretenders. Viewed as a business, it was a failing business. Viewed through the eyes of twenty-five-year-old Elizabeth, it was a business in need of a turnaround.

ROYAL FAMILIES, ROYAL PAIN

Today, the family affairs of the British monarchy are generally just that: *affairs*—a liaison here, an indiscretion there,

here a divorce, and there a naughty photo in a tabloid newspaper. During the early Renaissance, however, when Elizabeth's grandfather came to power, family "affairs" were rather more brutal and of considerably greater consequence. Henry Tudor, earl of Richmond, seized the throne of England on August 22, 1485, having defeated the Yorkist king, Richard III, on the field of battle at Bosworth. Doubtless at the time this seemed just another product of England's turbulent government, and few predicted that the Tudor dynasty would last long. After all, since 1399, when Richard II was forced to abdicate to Henry IV, England had been ruled by no fewer than six kings, who fought at least fifteen major battles over the throne.

Not that it was much of a throne. England was not just an island, it was *half* an island (for Scotland was a sovereign realm unto itself, albeit an unruly and wild one), offering poverty to most and feudal wealth to a few. The king amounted to little more than a warlord who had managed, however temporarily, to outmaneuver and beat down the other warlords. While England scraped and squabbled, the nations of continental Europe expanded and prospered, economically as well as culturally.

Nor had Henry Tudor, now Henry VII, wrested possession of that throne by virtue of anything very special about himself. He lacked charisma as well as conviction. More than anything, he happened to be in the right place at the right time when key noblemen had deserted the hapless and unpopular Richard III. Wisely, though, he made a good marriage in Elizabeth of York, thereby bringing together the two great rival families of England, the House of Lancaster and the House of York. The badge of the Lancastrians was a red rose and that of the Yorkists a white, so the devastating wars that ensued during 1455–85 were called the Wars of the Roses. Henry's marriage to Elizabeth ended them.

Not only had the Wars of the Roses ended, but England was at last recovering from the scourge of the mid-fourteenth-century black death, a plague that created, besides great terror and misery, a lasting economic depression. From a low of perhaps 2 million in 1400, the English population was now rapidly increasing and would reach 4 million by the end of the reign of Queen Elizabeth I. This population growth stimulated the English economy, especially the woolen cloth trade, as more people demanded more clothing. England's island isolation also began to give way during this period, as international trade developed, based mostly on woolen exports.

The new economy brought its share of serious problems, however, chief among which were generally rising prices, accelerating inflation, decline in real wages, and an abundance of debased coinage—coins minted of little gold and much base metal, whose intrinsic value had fallen below their face value. This latter problem, a by-product of inflation, put English merchants at an increasing disadvantage in international trade, because foreign creditors were reluctant to extend loans to merchants who would repay them in a debased currency, and because foreign producers began to demand nothing less than gold in return for goods exported to England. Worse, the continental nations had begun to exploit the riches of the New World, a vast new source of raw materials and gold. England, yet to set sail, was in danger of being squeezed out of the European economy.

These economic and demographic pressures created great social upheaval in England. During the depressed fourteenth century, land was abundant, rents were low, labor was in great demand, and wages, relative to the cost of living, were high. With increased population and production, land was now scarce and expensive, rents high, and the cost of living far outstripped wages. Paradoxically, despite an increase in population, the demand for labor actually declined, because landlords now turned away from labor-intensive crop farming to devote more of their land to sheep grazing, which required nothing more than a single shepherd and his dog. In the cities, merchants enjoyed increased opportunities, and in the country, the landed gentry prospered. But the yeoman farmer and the agricultural laborer, the largest segments of the English population, languished.

ELIZABETH'S FATHER

Henry VII died in 1509, leaving the kingdom to his eighteen-year-old son, Henry VIII. Although the youth's England now had more in common with the rest of Europe than the

England of his father, the nation's dependence on the wool trade kept the countryside more feudal—and, therefore, more backward and depressed—than most of the Continent. As Henry VIII matured, he seized the reins of government from his chief adviser, Thomas Wolsey, and his other ministers and began to involve England in international politics and international warfare. The cultured king also brought to England continental scholars, artists, and musicians, transforming a medieval royal court into an enlightened, albeit still modest, court of the Renaissance.

While Henry VIII brought to England a central government more powerful and efficient than ever before and a court richer in culture and learning, he also bequeathed to the kingdom unprecedented religious turmoil.

Shortly before he was crowned in 1509, Henry married the widow of his brother Arthur. By all accounts, his marriage to Catherine of Aragon was a happy one for almost two decades. By 1527, however, Henry was clearly obsessed with what he deemed Catherine's failure to produce a male heir (she had given birth to a daughter, the future Queen Mary I, in 1516). At this time, too, Henry had become enamored of the young and vivacious Anne Boleyn, a lady of the royal court. Citing Leviticus 20:21, which bars marriage to a brother's widow, Henry now argued that God would never permit male "issue" from his sinful union with Catherine. He commanded Wolsey to petition Pope Clement VII for a decree proclaiming the marriage to Catherine invalid and permitting Henry to remarry. The Pope resisted this on two counts. To begin with, it was he who, at Henry's request, had granted the dispensation that allowed him to marry his brother's widow in the first place. Now Henry was asking him, effectively, to admit that he had been wrong—something no head of the Catholic Church was eager to do. Second, the Pope relied heavily on the protection of the Holy Roman emperor and king of Spain Charles V, the nephew of Catherine of Aragon. Catherine did not want the annulment, and Clement was loath to offend and alienate Charles. He denied Wolsey's petition.

Henry went ahead with a divorce trial in 1529, but in the absence of a papal decree, the trial adjourned without decision. Enraged, the king dismissed Wolsey and, the following year, accused him of treason. Wolsey died in 1530, en route to face the king's charges. Two years later, Henry replaced Wolsey with the consummately devious Thomas Cromwell, who proposed a radical solution to Henry's marital woes: a complete break with Rome, which would replace the authority of the Pope with that of the Archbishop of Canterbury— who would surely grant the divorce. Henry pushed the necessary legislation through Parliament in 1533, divorced Catherine, married Anne Boleyn—and, yes, in the process created the Church of England, which during the next several years would bring the kingdom to the verge of civil war over the issue of religion.

Outwardly, the new Church of England seemed little different from the Roman Catholic Church. The mass was still conducted in Latin, and worship continued, essentially, as it had under Rome. On the one hand, this lessened the shock of—and, therefore, popular resistance to—the break with the Pope. On the other hand, it created great discontent among more committed Protestants who thought that many of the Catholic practices of worship and church government were corrupt and needed to be radically altered or abandoned entirely. Over the years, this position would create great confusion within the Church of England, would weaken it, and would generate bitter dissension throughout the realm.

For now, though, most of the dissension was centered on Henry's court. In September 1533, Anne Boleyn bore the king a daughter, Elizabeth, who was named heir to the throne in place of Catherine of Aragon's daughter, Mary. Indeed, the union with Catherine having been decreed illegal, Mary was declared a bastard. But Henry was left unsatisfied. Like Catherine before her, Anne "failed" to bring a male heir into the world. Henry persuaded himself that Anne had been unfaithful to him—an act of treason under English law—and she was executed in 1536. The union of Henry and a third wife, Jane Seymour, did produce a son, the sickly and frail Edward, who seemed destined for a brief life. After a difficult delivery, Jane herself soon died, and Henry took as his fourth wife Anne of Cleves in 1540. Anne, a solid, if plain, German Lutheran, held no allure for Henry, who divorced her almost immediately, charged the arranger of the marriage, Thomas Cromwell, with treason, and saw to his subsequent trial and execution.

Wife number five was Catherine Howard, whose youth and beauty made her a dramatic contrast to the homely Anne. Headstrong and impressionable—and doubtless physically repelled by the aging and obese Henry—Catherine had an affair with a courtier. She, too, was charged with, tried for, and convicted of treason, for which she was beheaded in 1542. More fortunate was the king's sixth wife, Catherine Parr, who managed a feat none of the others had achieved: widowhood.

BLOODY MARY

On the death of Henry VIII in 1547, nine-year-old Edward VI assumed the throne, under the regency of a "Protector," his uncle Edward Seymour, who was subsequently overthrown by the unscrupulous John Dudley, earl of Warwick and duke of Northumberland. During the half-dozen years of Edward's reign, the Protestant reformation proceeded in England with heightened intensity, which provoked a backlash from those who still clung to Catholic ways. On the death of Edward from tuberculosis at age sixteen, Northumberland staged an insurrection during July 6–19, 1553, in an attempt to put his daughter-in-law, Lady Jane Grey, on the throne in place of Mary. Mary was still officially illegitimate, but she, not Elizabeth, had been named in Henry VIII's will as his successor after Edward. Lady Jane reigned a mere nine days before the insurrection was crushed. Both Northumberland and Jane Grey were executed, and Mary I ascended the throne.

As early as 1549, Elizabeth had been suspected of plotting against Edward, and she now fell under suspicion of complicity with Dudley in the scheme to put Lady Jane on the throne. During most of Mary's reign, Elizabeth would be held under varying degrees of house arrest. Then, in 1554, Mary sent her to the Tower of London, believing she had conspired in an armed rebellion led by Thomas Wyatt of Kent. After two months, she was released—and was indeed fortunate to have escaped with her life. However, she could do little during her half-sister's reign except watch the queen tear the nation apart.

Animated by the Catholic faith she never renounced, and also moved by a desire to vindicate her mother's memory, Mary set about undoing the Protestant Reformation her father and Edward's government had begun. In 1554, she married Philip II of Spain, son of the Holy Roman emperor Charles V. She officially restored Roman Catholicism as the state religion, which outraged and terrified England's Protestants, yet did not even manage to gratify all of the nation's Catholics, many of whom deeply distrusted the Catholics of Philip's Spain. The union of Mary and Philip embroiled England in Spain's wars with France, the financing of which worked great hardship on the English people. The "foreign" wars were highly unpopular and divisive. The cruelest blow of all came in January 1558 when Calais, England's last possession on the European continent, fell to a French siege. ("When I am dead and opened," Mary is said to have remarked, "ye shall find Calais lying in my heart.")

At home, England lurched toward civil war over the ongoing reversal of the Reformation. Mary handled the situation with a complete lack of sensitivity or political savvy. To Protestant protest she responded with terror. From 1555 until her death in 1558, she caused some three hundred Protestant leaders to be burned at the stake as heretics. Others, untold hundreds of others, either fled or were exiled to the Continent. For all of this the queen earned the sobriquet of Bloody Mary.

But Mary's own greatest anguish did not come from involvement in European wars or religious turmoil at home. Its source was her inability to conceive a child. Late in her reign she finally showed certain signs of pregnancy—and was, for a time, ecstatic. But it soon became cruelly apparent that what was growing in her belly was no child. Mary succumbed to cancer, presumably of the ovaries, on November 17, 1558. She died unmourned, leaving to Elizabeth, still officially the bastard child of a traitor, a realm most unhappy.

"OH, LORD! THE QUEEN IS A WOMAN!"

When she was born at Greenwich Palace on September 7, 1533, the baby Elizabeth was a terrible disappointment to her father and mother, as any daughter would be in a royal family in which only boys really mattered. A boy, after all, could be a king, whereas a girl—well, a girl could be a queen, of course, but, as one flabbergasted citizen exclaimed when she first laid eyes on Queen Elizabeth shortly after her coronation, "Oh, Lord! The Queen is a woman!"

Yes, a girl could be a queen, but could she ever really govern a country? The fact was that women in Tudor England were regarded as little more than property and often were not treated with nearly as much care. Legal annals from this period mention the case of a man who, fined for mercilessly thrashing his servant, exclaimed that the world had arrived at a sorry state indeed and that the time would surely come when "a man might not even beat his own wife!"

Born a disappointment, Elizabeth grew up to face—and to survive—even worse. Her mother, Anne Boleyn, had been executed as an adulterous traitor, and Elizabeth herself declared a bastard. Throughout her childhood, Elizabeth was more or less exiled to Hatfield, an estate well away from the royal court. Her governess and tutors noted her great intelligence, her insatiable appetite for learning, and her precocious gravity of manner, better suited to a middle-aged woman than to a child. From age ten onward she spent much of her time with her half-brother, Edward, whom she certainly loved, and she was cared for kindly by her latest stepmother, Henry's last wife, Catherine Parr.

Almost immediately after Henry's death in 1547, Catherine Parr married Thomas Seymour, England's lord high admiral and a man who was handsome, dashing, ambitious, and utterly without scruples. With Henry out of the way, he immediately began scheming against his brother, Edward Seymour, regent ("Protector") to the ten-year-old Edward VI. In January 1549, shortly after Catherine Parr died, Edward Seymour moved against his scheming brother, charging him with a list of treasonous acts, not the least of which was plotting to marry young Elizabeth in order to assume control of the kingdom. After a trial, Thomas Seymour was executed, and Elizabeth fell under a blanket of suspicion, accused of having had a romantic and even sexual relationship with Seymour and of having participated in his plotting. Although nothing was ever proved against Elizabeth—indeed, it is unlikely that any of the suspicions had basis—she was kept under close watch. Knowing that her life was continually in danger, Elizabeth learned the arts of circumspection, of behaving in ways that betrayed nothing of what one was thinking, and generally of stealthy survival.

With the death of Edward VI in 1553 and the ascension of Mary I, Elizabeth found herself in even greater danger than before. She made it her business to conform outwardly and without protest to the Catholic rituals of worship. She professed loyalty and love to Mary. Yet she was continually under suspicion of plotting against her half-sister, was imprisoned for two months in the Tower of London, then was released to house arrest at Woodstock. After about a year, Elizabeth was freed—although she was always keenly aware of being observed. Doubtless, the emotional strain was great, but so was the opportunity to learn, practice, and perfect the skills of political, spiritual, and physical survival. This long, unhappy apprenticeship to the politics of dangerous compromise and sustained deception would serve her well when she became queen.

ELIZABETH TAKES CHARGE

Although none but the most ardent of Catholics mourned the passing of "Bloody Mary," many English men *and* women were distressed that rule had passed to yet another woman. But Elizabeth presented herself in a way that worked immediately to dispel the doubts. Tall and beautiful in the best tradition of courtly chivalry—fair, pale, her silken hair a fine, light reddish blond—she instantly demonstrated a charismatic rapport with the crowds that clogged the streets of London in celebration of the coronation. She came as the proverbial breath of fresh air, but not as a whirlwind. Through statements and symbolic gestures she made it clear that she meant to return England not only to the path of the Protestant Reformation, but to greatness in trade and among the nations.

She was careful not to act suddenly or sweepingly. Her childhood of danger and self-preserving self-restraint had taught her a kind of decisive patience. She would work to effect change slowly and in ways that would retain enough of the old to give everyone a measure of comfort and confidence. Moreover, while strong-willed and decisive, Elizabeth would gather about herself the best and brightest political and economic minds of England to be members of her inner circle of advisers, the Privy Council. Even here she was careful to retain on the council the best people from the reigns of her predecessors, including some ardent Catholics, judiciously adding to this number new councillors of her own choosing.

A WOMAN IN A MAN'S WORLD

Most people of Elizabeth's day took it for granted that women were not only intellectually and temperamentally unsuited to leadership, but morally incapable of it as well. Male leadership was consonant with the rule of God and nature. Female leadership was not. The new queen's answer to these objections was a combination of prudence, boldness, and genius.

The prudence we have just touched on. She surrounded herself with extraordinarily able advisers, chosen for their ability rather than out of personal affection. Moreover, Elizabeth skillfully blended advisers from the past with those of her own choosing, thereby creating a sense of continuity accompanied by change rather than sudden, discordant revolution.

The boldness was rooted in Elizabeth's style of command. She used her formidable intellect, shaped by years of tutelage under some of the most able minds of her age, to make herself absolute mistress of the facts impacting on her realm: the political situation, the economic situation, the religious situation. She used her equally formidable ability to read human character—again, a faculty developed by necessity during the perilous years of her upbringing when every friend was a potential enemy—as a tool to penetrate and analyze the needs, desires, and intentions of those around her. Armed with a wealth of information and insight, Elizabeth issued decisive, even imperious commands. She took a buck-stops-here approach to leadership, framed in bold statements and expressed through bold actions—except when it suited her to buy time or deliberately delay definitive action. The style was personal and intense.

Finally came the genius. All effective leaders appreciate the power of image, and they strive, to greater or lesser degrees, to develop about themselves an image of leadership suited to the psychology of those they lead. Elizabeth deeply understood the culture from which she and her people sprung. As far as women were concerned, this culture favored two convergent ideals. The glamorous lore of chivalry and the courtly tradition painted the feminine ideal as the virgin, pale, fair of hair, and of willowy, ethereal figure. Concurrently, the religion of Roman Catholicism worshiped the Blessed Virgin not only as the mother of God, but as a kind of goddess herself, a being who could intercede for those who prayed to her, and a proper object of worship in her own right. Elizabeth recognized that a weakness of Protestantism, as far as the emotional life of the people were concerned, was its diminishment of the role of the Blessed Virgin. To be sure, she was still to be venerated as Christ's mother, but she was no longer to be set between the faithful and God as a kind of intermediate object of worship. Grasping that this "removal" of the Virgin had left a hungry void in the Protestant heart, Elizabeth began to develop about herself—in her appearance, her conduct, her every pronouncement—the image of a Virgin Queen, at once a blend of the courtly ideal and the religious one. If the absence of the Blessed Virgin had created an empty place in Protestant England's emotions, Elizabeth herself would fill it. Thus the queen portrayed herself—and allowed others to portray her—as an earthly incarnation of the Virgin.

This self-created image carried a bonus and a burden for Elizabeth. The undercurrent drama of her long reign would always be the issue of marriage and the creation of an undisputed heir to the throne. Parliament repeatedly pressured her to wed, and Elizabeth repeatedly evaded the subject—allowing a series of prospective husbands to court her without committing to any of them and, remarkably, without alienating most of them. The virgin image gave her an *excuse* for her refusal to marry even as the necessity of maintaining that increasingly valuable image dictated that she *must not* marry.

WEDDED TO ENGLAND

Through the long years since Elizabeth's passing, many commentators have speculated on what deep psychological barrier, what secret wound of the heart, prevented Elizabeth from taking a husband. Elizabeth herself had a simple answer: She did not want to diminish her power by placing a husband above her. Moreover, any husband she might choose would carry with him into the marriage as much liability as benefit. Marrying a foreign prince might create a desired alliance, but it would also entangle England in that alliance, as Mary's union with Philip II had dragged the nation into Spain's war with France. Marrying an Englishman would create among the nobility as many jealousies and enmities as it would garner staunch supporters.

Of course, in the absence of marriage, one grave problem remained necessarily unresolved: the matter of succession. The passing of each monarch was a dangerous time for English government, a time of instability and potential revolution. Without a clearly designated heir to the throne, this time was made all the more hazardous. If Elizabeth would not marry and give birth to a natural heir, then Parliament pressured her at least to designate a successor. But this Elizabeth refused to do throughout her reign. She understood that naming a successor would tempt the one selected and his partisans to seize power prematurely, while, on the other hand, it would alienate those who had been passed over, tempting them and their adherents to rebellion. Thus, with great aplomb, she purposely evaded the issue of the royal succession throughout a reign that spanned more than four decades.

LESSONS IN LEADERSHIP

In the chapters that follow, you will read how, through a reign of forty-five years, Elizabeth time and again transformed crises into opportunities, almost always by taking a positive but moderate course. Nowhere was this more evident than in her handling of religion, an area in which she enforced orthodoxy but not at the expense of personal conscience or conviction, and in her canny coping with her chief rival for the throne, her cousin Mary, Queen of Scots.

Using the queen's own words whenever possible, each chapter in this book presents concise narrative examples of leadership in crisis and triumph. Together, these episodes tell the story of a woman who faced grave dangers, formidable challenges, and spectacular opportunities, and who managed all of them to her advantage as well as to the benefit of her nation. She was, of course, an exceptional leader. Yet her experience speaks to leaders of all enterprises in any age and in any place. For the businessperson in particular, charged with making the most of limited resources to address effectively the divergent demands and needs of subordinates, bosses, customers, and investors, Elizabeth's story is especially eloquent and revelatory. We will follow the queen as she leads her nation

- through crisis and confrontation with foreign powers in Scotland and on the continent;
- through economic disaster to economic growth and triumph;
- in the defense of the beleaguered Huguenots, the Protestants of France;
- in the exploration of the New World;
- in aid of the Republic of the Netherlands against the oppressive yoke of Spain;
- in remarkably effective combat against Spain on the high seas;
- in the defense of England against the Spanish Armada and the threat of invasion;
- in building the foundation of a great British empire and an even greater English culture of literature, art, learning, and enduringly sound government.

Each chapter and each episode within each chapter is self-contained and, it is hoped, self-explanatory; however, the exploration of events more than four centuries old does require a limbering of the historical imagination. You may find it helpful to refer to the "Elizabethan Chronicle" that forms the appendix of this book. It will fill you in on the background context of key events in Tudor times. You are also invited to review the list of Recommended Reading at the back of the book. The works listed there have served as the primary sources for *Elizabeth I, CEO*. They have much to teach us, for the life of Elizabeth and the culture of the era to which she gave her name are sufficiently rich to reward a lifetime of study.

Much suspected by me,
Nothing proved can be,
Quoth Elizabeth, prisoner.

—Verse scratched into a
windowpane at Woodstock by Elizabeth
while under house arrest during 1554

One

"MY LITTLE POWER"

A LEADER'S FIRST LESSON: SURVIVAL

A *LEADER'S FIRST DUTY IS SURVIVAL. FOR MOST TYPICAL managers or CEOs this means nothing more or less than keeping your job. For Elizabeth it meant that and more. It meant staying alive, keeping her neck off the block on which her mother's had already lain. Even in later years, when she had outlived her early adversaries and was queen of England, physical survival and the maintenance of strength, good health, and a calm, clear mind remained important issues for Elizabeth, as they are for any leader. This chapter presents Elizabeth, first and foremost, as a survivor.*

1. CHERISH CORE VALUES
"The Mind I Shall Never Be Ashamed to Present"

When Elizabeth was thirteen, an anonymous portrait painter at Windsor Palace produced a likeness of her, which she presented to her sister, Queen Mary I. In a letter accompanying the Windsor portrait, young Elizabeth wrote: "For the face I grant I might well blush to offer, but the mind I shall never be ashamed to present." She continued: "For though from the grace of the picture the colours may fade by time, may give [deteriorate] by weather, may be spotted by chance, yet the other, nor time with her swift wings shall overtake, nor misty clouds with their lowerings may darken, nor chance with her slippery foot may overthrow."

Elizabeth learned at an early age that outward, superficial things—including all the trappings of power—are fragile, transitory, subject to destruction even by trivial accident. The inner truths, however, may be far more substantial and enduring. The portrait Elizabeth gave to her sister shows her holding a book of devotions and standing beside another book. In her letter, Elizabeth seeks to direct her sister's attention away from the superficial—the face—and to what the books represent: the mind, the inner life.

But there is more. Give some thought to Elizabeth's declaration that she "shall never be ashamed to present" her mind. It amounts to a resolution to formulate enduring, honorable principles and to remain devoted to them even in the "face" of changing superficialities. From an early age Elizabeth had grasped the importance of leadership anchored in a firm mental position—not just from a set of principles arbitrarily or conveniently chosen, but from the workings of a "mind," of which one need never be ashamed.

Historians tell us that a major difference between the medieval and renaissance worlds is that the former was characterized by changelessness, whereas the latter was typified by change. If medieval people groveled in their villages and holed up in their castles, renaissance people vigorously traded with one another and traveled across the ocean to a New World. Today, of course, business is characterized by a pervasive dynamism. Things change. Stock traders who used to buy and hold a stock, perhaps for years, now buy and sell in a day, an hour, even a minute. The prices of commodities rise and fall in a heartbeat. A deal is proposed in the morning, withdrawn before lunch, and revived by dinnertime.

What can you hold on to?

At age thirteen, Elizabeth already knew.

2. SURVIVAL IS NEVER ABOUT PANIC
Keeping Your Head

Turn to any recent management text, and you'll read a lot about "team building," "collegiality," "supportiveness," "sensitivity," and "mentoring." What you won't find are words like "fear" and "intimidation." But the fact is that these are all too real dimensions of management. At some time or other, someone above you will bring a certain pressure to bear: the threat of a descending axe, the thud of a skull, and the echo of rolling heads.

For us, of course, all of this is just metaphor.

"Watch out! Heads will roll!" we say.

"I do *not* want to walk into my boss's office and hand him my head," we say.

"Well, your you-know-what may be in a sling, but *my* head's on the block," we say.

In Elizabeth's England, metaphors were for poets and playwrights like Edmund Spenser and William Shakespeare. Kings and queens didn't need metaphors. They held all the axes.

So when Elizabeth, age sixteen, found herself implicated in the schemes of the freshly beheaded Thomas Seymour, accused of dalliance with him, and accused of having plotted with him against her half-brother, Edward VI, she had plenty to worry about.

The young king's Protector, Edward Seymour, the very man who had just sent his own brother Thomas on the way to the chopping block, dispatched the imposing Sir Thomas Tyrwhitt to interrogate the teenage girl. Others close to her had already been arrested and sent to the infamous Tower of London, which often served as the executioner's waiting room. Tyrwhitt believed it would be an easy matter to intimidate young Elizabeth, to wring from her either a confession on her own account or material that would incriminate the other prisoners, which included her "cofferer" (household manager), Sir Thomas Parry, and her beloved governess, Katherine ("Kat") Ashley.

Tyrwhitt grilled Elizabeth relentlessly for days, but, in a letter of January 23, 1549, he confessed something like defeat at her hands: "She hath a very good wit and nothing is got out of her but by great policy. . . . She will not confess any practice by Mrs. Ashley or the cofferer."

Elizabeth knew how to keep her head. It was not by defiance, but by strength of character, a refusal to be intimidated, and a choice never to panic. These qualities were already present and had been sorely tested in her. As she grew into adulthood, she seemed deliberately to cultivate, nurture, and practice resistance to intimidation and avoidance of panic. Did she understand that these qualities would not only save her life, but would also be necessary to the life of a leader who would save her nation and see it prosper?

Perhaps.

But what we must derive from Elizabeth's example is the lesson that a leader must learn to keep her head—and the earlier the better. For the axe is mighty sparing of second chances.

3. CONTROL THE MESSAGE, NOT THE MESSENGER
Kill Rumors, Not People

Elizabeth was sixteen, her governess and her household manager (cofferer) jailed in the Tower of London, her flirtatious friend and would-be fiancé under indictment for treason, and she herself under the gravest suspicion. Already, the rumor mill was grinding: She had plotted with Thomas Seymour, it was said, to put him in line for the throne; she had slept with Thomas Seymour, it was said, and was pregnant by him.

Sir Edward Seymour, Thomas Seymour's brother and chief accuser, promised Elizabeth that anyone who slandered her would be severely punished. It must have been a very reassuring and inviting promise. Picture the young girl, flirtatious herself, perhaps, but innocent of the charges floating about her. Having been raised to value honor and honesty above all else, it was precisely these qualities that were now being called into question. If the slanderous rumors were allowed to take root, Elizabeth's reputation would be ruined. And that was the best-case scenario. Worst case? The Lady Elizabeth would follow in her mother's footsteps to the grim block in the courtyard of the Tower of London.

But even in this extreme crisis, Elizabeth retained her presence of mind, showing an extraordinary understanding of how public opinion works.

Edward Seymour had pledged to punish slanderers and rumormongers. All Elizabeth need do was report their names to him. Elizabeth wrote a letter in reply. She told Edward Seymour that if she did report the slanderers, this "should be but a breeding of an evil name of me, that I am glad to punish them, and so get the evil will of the people, which thing I loth to have."

Think about it. Offered an opportunity for instant vengeance against those who spoke ill of her, Elizabeth declined—not out of faintheartedness but because she instinctively understood that complaining about others and getting them in trouble would ultimately backfire *on her*. It might silence a few loose tongues, but it would, if anything, further spread the evil message and, what is worse, both amplify it and, in the minds of the people, confirm its truth.

Vengeance, Elizabeth reasoned, was not the way to scotch a rumor or shape public opinion. But Elizabeth also knew that rumors could not be ignored. They had to be dealt with positively, aggressively, and swiftly. After asking Edward Seymour to refrain from punishing the slanderers, she continued in her letter: "But if it might seem good unto your Lordship and the rest of the council to send forth a proclamation into the counties that they restrain their tongues declaring how the tales are but lies, it should make both the people think that you and the council have great regard that no such rumours should be spread of any King's Majesty's Sisters . . ."

The suggested course of action is not only effective but brilliantly expressed. Let's take a closer look at it:

1. Elizabeth frames her request as a *request*, not a demand. She expresses it as a proposal to be judged by Edward Seymour and the council: "if it might seem good unto your Lordship and the rest of the council." Persuasive people—the "closers" of deals—never impose, never browbeat. Instead, they present their point of view so that it becomes the point of view of the person they wish to persuade. Do you want to sell an idea? Begin by making the prospective "customer" believe the idea is already his.

2. Elizabeth proposes a *positive* action. Her object is not to punish those who spread rumors but to stop the rumors.

Punishment will stop the work of a few rumormongers, but it will not stop the rumors; indeed, Elizabeth reasons, punishment, a *negative* action, will only intensify the "evil will of the people." A proclamation calling for restraint and proclaiming the rumors untrue punishes no one but does put an official end to the tales.

3. Elizabeth proposes action by someone else. The shy among us are frequently told that we have to toot our own horn. Nevertheless, it is far more effective to get someone else to do the tooting. It's one thing to sing your own praises but quite another to have others sing them for you. Similarly, you can defend yourself against gossip, but it is far more effective to have others declare the gossip untrue. This is precisely what Elizabeth proposes.

4. Elizabeth appeals to a good beyond herself. Most of us dislike asking for favors. Doubtless, Elizabeth felt the same way. She does not ask Edward Seymour to help *her* but to help her as one of "any of the King's Majesty's Sisters." Edward Seymour's job is the king's Protector. In effect, she asks him to do his job by now protecting the king's sister.

Elizabeth closes this letter with the phrase "Written in haste from Hatfield this 21 of February." Yet there is nothing hasty at all about the letter, which is carefully thought out in terms of proportioning means to ends, the remedy to the problem.

4. KNOWLEDGE REALLY IS POWER
A Leader Learns

Intellect is a gift, but learning is hard work. From an early age Elizabeth made it her business to learn all that she could. Her object was to fashion herself into an enlightened princess who might well come to rule the nation. Her education was typical of the best the Renaissance had to offer, but it was highly unusual for a girl. She became fluent in the classical languages, Latin and the more difficult Greek. As her tutor Robert Ascham wrote, "She readeth more Greek every day than some Prebendaries of this Church do in a whole week." Her immediate object was to enable herself to speak intelligently with anyone on any intellectual topic, and this included the course of human and political events. As a child and young woman she spent at least three hours a day reading history. Even when she went out walking, she would take along a book, which she tucked into a pouch that hung from her girdle.

5. LEARN THE TRANSCENDENT VALUE OF LOYALTY
"When Your Need Shall Be the Most You Shall Find My Friendship Greatest"

When Edward VI died of tuberculosis at age sixteen in 1553, Elizabeth's half-sister, Mary, assumed the throne. A Catholic, her ascension threw fear and confusion into the newly

Protestant realm. Mary and her advisers immediately moved to consolidate and protect her power. Parliament quickly declared the marriage of her mother, Catherine of Aragon, and Henry VIII lawful (Henry had engineered its annulment) and, therefore, the subsequent marriage of Henry and Anne Boleyn unlawful. Thus, in a stroke, Elizabeth was confirmed a bastard, and she was publicly humiliated. The ruling council, however, continued to uphold Elizabeth's rights as heiress to the throne. Mary was furious and fearful; even bastardized, her sister continued to loom as a threat. Mary remarked that Elizabeth was bound to become like her mother: a woman "who had caused great trouble in the Kingdom."

Terrified and depressed, the young Elizabeth nevertheless refused to wallow in self-pity. When her cousin, Lady Katherine Knollys, the daughter of Anne Boleyn's sister, decided to leave the hostility of the royal court, Elizabeth wrote to wish her well, pledging that "when your need shall be the most you shall find my friendship greatest. Let others promise, and I will do, in words not more in deeds as much."

Elizabeth would never feel more powerless than she felt now. Indeed, she would never be more powerless. Yet she gathered up what power had been left to her—her friendship, her love, her loyalty—and pledged it to another in need. Sooner or later, all enduring leaders learn the transcendent value of loyalty. Elizabeth learned it sooner, and she would never forget or forsake it.

6. USE ALL THE POWER YOU HAVE
Without Panic

The year after she succeeded Edward VI, Queen Mary I wed Philip II of Spain, son of the Holy Roman emperor Charles V. The marriage—to a foreigner and a Catholic—greatly intensified political unrest in England. Not only were Protestants fearful of persecution, but many English Catholics were also disturbed, for they distrusted the Catholics of Spain. In contrast to the queen Elizabeth would one day prove to be, Mary showed little regard for political reality. She wished to marry Philip, and so she did, heedless of the consequences.

Shortly before Mary's wedding, in an atmosphere of increasing political upheaval, Sir Thomas Wyatt led a rebellion in Kent and marched on London. There, however, the insurrection collapsed, and Wyatt, along with other rebels, was sentenced to death. The charge against him, specifically, was plotting to overthrow Mary and replace her with Elizabeth. In fact, Elizabeth had played no role in Wyatt's rebellion, but Mary chose to believe in her probable guilt. She ordered her half-sister transported to the Tower of London.

Elizabeth, at this time overwrought, was so ill that her doctors told Mary she could not be moved. Pitiless now, Mary concluded that Elizabeth was playacting, and she ordered the young woman to be brought to London in a litter.

There can be no doubt that Elizabeth was terrified to be following the very path her mother, Anne Boleyn, had trod.

Yet she refused to give in to her panic. While being carried in her enclosed litter through the streets of London, she dramatically threw back the vehicle's curtains so that all the city could see how sick she was and how cruelly she was being treated.

Transferred to a boat for delivery to the Tower of London, the very prison that had held her mother prior to her execution, the twenty-one-year-old had every reason to panic. She was a prisoner. She was powerless.

Or was she?

To have panicked would indeed have been to concede powerlessness and, in so doing, would have relinquished what little power Elizabeth still commanded in this dire situation. However, the young woman realized that if she remained calm, she could exploit her imprisonment symbolically. Disembarking from the boat that took her down the Thames in the rain to the Tower's infamous Watergate, portal of the condemned, Elizabeth did not cry or protest but simply declared, "Here landeth as true a subject, being prisoner, as ever landed at these stairs." With that, she sat down on the flagstones before the entrance to the Tower. When the lieutenant of the Tower pleaded with her to come in out of the rain, Elizabeth replied, "It is better sitting here than in a worse place." At this, one of Elizabeth's gentlemen ushers broke down in tears. Instead of following suit, Elizabeth turned sternly and told him (according to a witness) that she "knew her truth to be such that no man would have cause to weep for her." Having regained some of the initiative by this declaration, she at last entered the Tower—doing so, in effect, on her own terms.

Defeat is always a possibility. But a large part of defeat consists in admitting defeat. When others attempt to defeat you, there is always the hope that they will fail and you will prevail. If you admit defeat, you are defeated. The deal is done, period. There is, therefore, no advantage in yielding to panic and trumpeting your own defeat. If your power has been reduced, use what little power is left to you. Keep your potential alive.

7. FIRST: STAY ALIVE
A Duty to Survive

Under house arrest at Woodstock, after her release from the Tower of London, Elizabeth could do little except survive. What little she *could* do, she was determined *to* do.

On November 27, 1554, it was announced that Queen Mary I was pregnant. Shortly thereafter, her husband, Philip II, wrote to the Pope to describe the return of England to the Roman Catholic faith. Almost immediately, Parliament reenacted the heresy laws, making it a capital crime to profess the Protestant religion. Those who openly practiced Protestantism could be burned at the stake. As it turned out, Mary's pregnancy was false—probably a symptom of the ovarian cancer that would claim her life in 1558—but the Counter-Reformation had been set into motion, and Mary began to earn the epithet by which she became known to history:

Bloody Mary. During her reign, some three hundred Protestant leaders were executed, most by torture and burning.

Elizabeth, who during this dark period habitually (and truthfully) signed her letters "Your assured friend to my little power," did her duty. Outwardly, she worshiped as a Catholic, and she refrained from criticizing her sister in the least.

Was this dishonest? To worship what you do not feel is, by definition, a lie. But it was a matter of living from day to day in the hope that circumstances would be improved. Going with the flow, riding out a storm, behaving in a manner that is necessary rather than fully truthful is among the hardest things a leader may have to do. The fact is that there is no such thing as a dead leader.

8. KEEP A CLEAR HEAD
AND AN EVEN KEEL
Calming Down

Elizabeth rarely allowed herself to become overwrought. She found that translating Latin or Greek texts had a calming effect on her, and as one of her godchildren, Sir John Harington, observed, "She was wont to soothe her ruffled temper with reading every morning." Elizabeth also found an outlet in vigorous physical exercise, especially in long, brisk walks. During tense negotiations, she would sometimes leave the room to walk in the garden, returning after a time, fully calmed and ready to continue.

9. DON'T BE SO QUICK
TO BREAK THE EGG
Close to the Vest

While Elizabeth put a great premium on her word and on keeping her word—the "word of a Prince," as she called it—she was also master of creative deceit. This did not extend to outright falsehood but to a habit of playing it close to the vest, never fully revealing her hand and frequently keeping her true feelings hidden. This is always a risky way of conducting business, but it was well suited to the complex world of Tudor politics. A leader must remember that once all secrets are revealed, the egg is broken and can't be made whole again. Sometimes one has to be parsimonious with information and purposefully reluctant to reveal the full extent of one's feelings.

10. THE REWARDS OF
MODERATION
Strong Drink

Drinking the water in Elizabeth's day could be hazardous to your health. Typically, there was little if any separation between water supply systems and sewage systems. Understandably, then, the drink of choice was not water, but wine or beer. Elizabeth, according to courtier Edmund Bohun, "seldom drank above three times at a meal, and that was common beer." While she enjoyed wine, she rarely drank it because she feared that it would cloud her faculties.

Elizabeth was no ascetic, but she did believe in moderation, both as a demonstration of sound judgment and as an aid to achieving and maintaining it.

11. ALWAYS PLAY A MOVE AHEAD
The Game

The French ambassador had an audience with Elizabeth while she was engrossed in a game of chess. "This game," the ambassador suavely observed, "is an image of the works and deeds of men. If we lose a pawn it seems a small matter; but the loss often brings with it that of the whole game." Elizabeth replied: "I understand you. Darnley is only a pawn but he may checkmate me if he is promoted."

Her reference was to Lord Darnley, whom Mary, Queen of Scots was destined to wed. (See Chapter Eight for the story of Mary, Queen of Scots.) Elizabeth believed that Darnley posed little threat to her unless he did marry her rival and thereby enjoyed "promotion," like a pawn that reaches the last rank of the chessboard.

Elizabeth fully appreciated the dynamic, even fluid nature of power: how royal inheritance might make it seem as if fortune and authority were foregone conclusions, but circumstances could readily change everything overnight. Elizabeth knew that her own mother, for example, was queen one day, an adjudged traitor the next, and a corpse soon after. She saw her own fortune change with the deaths of Edward VI and her half-sister, Mary I. She understood well that a leader cannot stand apart from the game but must actively engage in it, always mastering the changing chessboard, always standing ready to respond to a new challenge from a "piece" once thought inconsiderable and powerless.

12. NEVER UNDERCUT YOURSELF
"The Head Should Not Be Subject to the Foot"

Throughout much of her reign, Elizabeth was keenly aware of the ongoing threat posed by Mary, Queen of Scots (see Chapter Eight, pp. 187–199). A substantial number of Catholics in England wanted nothing more than to dethrone Protestant Elizabeth and replace her with Catholic Mary. Nevertheless, Elizabeth repeatedly and for years acted to protect and preserve Mary's life while also containing her. Typical is Elizabeth's response to the action of the Scottish Lords of the Congregation, which staged a rebellion against Mary after the mysterious murder of her husband, Lord Darnley. Elizabeth conveyed this message to the Lords:

> *You may assure them we so detest and abhor the murder*
> *committed upon our cousin [Darnley], their King, and*
> *mislike as much as any of them the marriage of the Queen*
> *our sister [Mary, Queen of Scots] with Bothwell [who was*

suspected of complicity in the murder of Darnley]. But herein we dissent from them, that we think it is not lawful nor tolerable for them, being by God's ordinance subjects, to call her, who also by God's ordinance is their superior and Prince, to answer to their accusations by way of force. We do not think it consonant in nature that the head should be subject to the foot.

As Elizabeth understood the world, the ultimate basis of her power and authority was the same as Mary's: "God's ordinance." To countenance a rebellion against Mary would be to approve an attack on the system that supported them both. Elizabeth refused to jeopardize that system even though it would have been most convenient to rid herself of her rival once and for all. A leader must know when to work within the system and when, if ever, to depart from it. Certainly, a leader must avoid acting in reckless or impulsive ways that ultimately undermine his own authority even if immediate gains may be made by such action.

13. BE SURE YOU'LL WIN
Test of Loyalty

Many of us raised on Hollywood westerns—and variations thereon—have an unfortunate weakness for showdowns. We like the idea of the make-or-break contest that settles an issue once and for all, such as the gun duel in *High Noon*.

Sometimes a showdown is, in fact, called for. There are issues that fester if they are not definitively and quickly resolved. But before you force a showdown, be certain that the outcome will go your way. If you are not certain, the better course may be a few deft sidesteps.

Parliament, in 1570, passed a series of bills to suppress Catholic worship practices in England. Elizabeth, of course, was intent on promoting uniformity of worship according to Anglican practice. Yet she had doubts about one of the bills that was passed. It made the taking of communion mandatory at least once a year and levied a heavy fine on those who failed to do so. Elizabeth ultimately vetoed the measure. It would have exposed what might be called closet Catholics—actually called, in Elizabeth's day, "Church Papists"—who were willing to attend Anglican divine service all year, but, when it came to Anglican communion, demurred.

Elizabeth did not want to force this showdown. If the bill prompted a precise count of Church Papists versus true-blue Anglicans, who would end up the winner and who the loser? Elizabeth was not certain, and because she was not certain, she vetoed the bill.

14. WEIGH THE RISKS
Answer to a Massacre

France, like England, was torn by civil strife between Protestants and Catholics. The French court attempted to resolve the conflict by arranging a marriage between the daughter of Catherine de Médicis (mother of Charles IX, king of France) and Henry, the Protestant king of Navarre. Among the guests who went to Paris to celebrate the wedding was Admiral Coligny, a prominent Huguenot (French Protestant) leader. On August 22, 1572, the admiral was assaulted and shot in the hand. Although Charles IX announced that the perpetrators would be found and punished, the Huguenots of Paris began to talk about taking vengeance of their own. Panic immediately spread throughout the French court and the city of Paris. On August 23, 1572, the eve of Saint Bartholomew's Day, Catherine de Médicis ordered the city cleared of Huguenots. Her son the king agreed, albeit reluctantly.

Historians have long argued whether Catherine, in effect, ordered the massacre that followed during August 24–25 or whether she simply wanted the Huguenots peaceably removed to preserve order. Whatever her intention, the Roman Catholic nobles of her court—together with others— did perpetrate a well-planned massacre, beginning with Coligny himself and other prominent Huguenots and then continuing with attacks on Huguenot homes and shops. Even after a royal order was issued on August 25 to stop the killing, more blood was shed in Paris, and the massacre spread to the provinces, including the towns of Rouen, Lyons, Bourges, Orléans, and Bordeaux. Estimates of the number of Huguenot dead vary from two thousand (this was the contemporary Catholic estimate) to seventy thousand (estimated by the Huguenot duke de Sully). Most modern historians believe that at least three thousand were killed in Paris alone.

The Catholic world responded with jubilation to news of the massacre. Philip II of Spain and Pope Gregory XIII had a medal struck to commemorate the event. Protestant nations, however, were horrified. Yet Elizabeth reacted rather mildly. She responded to the accusation that the Huguenots were attacked because they had plotted treason by remarking that they should not have been victimized but, rather, "brought to answer by law and to judgement before they were executed." Giving the law into the hands of the mob was, she said, a "terrible and dangerous example." Moreover, she expected Charles to be "more humane and noble." That he was not, she said, "increased our grief and sorrow in our good Brother's behalf."

But why didn't Elizabeth respond to the massacre with greater outrage?

Quite simply, she could not afford to wreck a delicate alliance with France. If she did, England would be vulnerable to combined attack from France and Spain, both Catholic nations.

It must have pained the queen greatly to restrain herself from expressing the outrage the massacre merited. But as a leader of a nation, she had to put the needs of that nation ahead of her own feelings, no matter how intense. She even consented to stand godmother to Charles's child, something to which she had happily agreed before the massacre.

Among the most difficult, sometimes even painful, things a leader does is push her personal feelings to the background when greater, collective issues are at stake.

15. YOUR SOURCES: THE CLOSER, THE BETTER
Firsthand

Elizabeth was notoriously impatient with long-winded sermons. Why? She explained that she would "rather talk with God devoutly by prayer than hear others speak eloquently of God." Like most creative leaders, Elizabeth wanted to get as close to the source—of knowledge, of inspiration, of power—as possible. She had no desire to take her religion at second hand even from the most learned of clergymen.

16. COURAGE ALWAYS COMMUNICATES
Guts

Elizabeth possessed both moral and physical courage, the courage of her convictions, the courage to take responsibility for her decisions, and the courage to face death. Assassination talk was frequently heard at court, and she was several times the target of attempts on her life. One day, while she was boating on the Thames near Greenwich, a man in another boat took a shot at her, wounding one of the royal oarsmen. Without hesitation—and without fear of a second shot—Elizabeth leaped forward to the wounded man, tore off her scarf, and used it to bind his wound, in the meantime assuring him to fear not, that she would take care of him.

In her later years, Elizabeth slept with a sword beside her bed.

She came in a cloud of dust and a shimmer of gold. Sitting regally in her gilded coach, resplendent in silk and brocade, jewels at her throat and in her hair, she appeared "like a goddess such as painters are wont to depict."

—CAROLLY ERICKSON,
in The First Elizabeth *(1983), describing the approach of Elizabeth's coach on a visit to a country village*

Two

FROM BASTARD CHILD TO VIRGIN QUEEN

CREATING A LEADERSHIP IMAGE

L EADERSHIP IS A COMPLEX COMPOUND OF ACTION AND *image. Elizabeth began life as a bastard outcast, barely able to hold on to life. Made queen, she worked quickly to transform the image of her identity from a daughter of sin to the Virgin Queen. In the process, she created one of history's most effective images of leadership.*

17. CREATE YOUR SELF-IMAGE—OR OTHERS WILL CREATE ONE FOR YOU
The Virgin Queen

All her life Elizabeth devoted much energy and wit to avoiding and evading marriage. Generations of historians, biographers, and psychologists (both professional and amateur) have speculated on the queen's motives for remaining not only single but, as far as anyone can determine, a virgin life-long. Certainly, one is tempted to look for motivation no further than her own highly dysfunctional family: her father wed six times, her mother killed at his behest, and a mean and mean-spirited half-sister who held her life in the palm of her hand. But it is also necessary to look beyond psychological motives to political ones: Elizabeth was simply unwilling to relinquish any of her power, authority, and freedom of action to a man. Furthermore, any choice of husband she made would create at least as many problems as it might solve. To wed a foreigner would entangle England in constraining alliances and would almost certainly bring religious conflict. To marry an Englishman would create jealousies and factionalism.

For whatever reasons, having chosen a solo course, Elizabeth made the most of her status as a virgin. In renaissance culture, virginity in women was a courtly ideal that automatically entailed comparisons with the Blessed Virgin Mary. To maintain oneself as a virgin was considered a kind of holy calling as well as a romantic one. Elizabeth understood that this in itself would appeal to the imagination of her courtiers and other government officials—even those who were deeply concerned about the absence of heirs to the throne. But Elizabeth also had the common people in mind. She ruled over a country that was in the throes of a religious revolution. In turning from Roman Catholicism to Anglican

Protestantism, one of the aspects of worship that was being cast substantially in the background was the Virgin Mary. Catholics of Elizabeth's day were devoted to the Virgin, even as they are today. In Protestant practice, the Virgin was still venerated but was no longer so intense a focus of worship. In a stroke of insightful genius, Elizabeth realized that her own virginity could fill the void that the absence of the Virgin Mary had created in the people's hearts. Certainly, Elizabeth did not set herself before her subjects as a god or goddess, but she did present herself as a new virgin, a virgin for a Protestant realm.

She allowed courtiers and poets to celebrate her as the "Virgin Queen." When Sir Walter Raleigh sought permission to name in her honor his patent territory in the New World, it was Elizabeth who suggested "Virginia." And when the poet Edmund Spenser wrote his epic verse romance *The Faerie Queene* (1590–1599), Elizabeth approved of how he had transformed her into a spiritual and mythological figure.

Physically, Elizabeth also took steps to enhance her image as an ageless, semidivine virgin. Renaissance ideals of female beauty called for very fair, even pallid skin and light blond hair (Elizabeth's was light reddish blond). Elizabeth enthusiastically exaggerated her own fair features to suit this ideal and even carried this to an extreme. An outdoorswoman who loved to ride and hunt, she often protected herself from the effects of the sun by wearing a mask, which she held in place by a button gripped between her teeth. She whitened her skin by applying powder made of ground alabaster. She also used lotions consisting of beeswax, ass's milk, and even the ground jawbones of hogs. It is likely that she took even more drastic whitening measures, which included application of a substance compounded of white lead and vinegar and another mixture consisting of borax and sulfur. To redden her lips in pleasing contrast to the artificial pallor of her complexion, she may have used a popular concoction of red ocher and red crystalline mercuric sulfide, as well as cochineal, a red dye made from the ground-up bodies of the scaly red cochineal insect. Most likely she did even more. Renaissance women routinely bleached freckles and other "blemishes" with a mixture of birch tree sap, ground brimstone (sulfur), oil of turpentine, and sublimate of mercury. In time, such preparations left the skin almost in a state of mummification. To disguise this, a glaze of egg white was applied, creating a sort of marblelike appearance. The eyelids were darkened with applications of kohl (antimony sulfide), and even the pupils of the eyes were exaggerated by applications of belladonna, which caused them to dilate. Nor was cosmetic dentistry neglected. Abrasive preparations such as pumice powder or ground coral were applied as whitening agents. Women even resorted to rubbing the teeth with nitric acid—called aqua fortis, or strong water, in Elizabeth's day.

Portraits of the mature Elizabeth make it clear that she used at least some of these cosmetic methods to fashion herself into the ideal of renaissance virginity, strongly suggesting a secular stand-in for the Virgin of the Roman Catholics.

Elizabeth understood what too few leaders understand today: that image counts, and not just in a superficial way. A leader is a flesh-and-blood human being, a thinker, and a decision maker, but he or she is also a profound symbol, the embodiment of the entire enterprise. Elizabeth understood herself in this regard, and she devoted much effort to styling and perfecting her image. The message she sent was powerful and unambiguous. No leader of a serious enterprise can afford to neglect the shaping of an effective and powerful image that promotes the cohesiveness of the organization and the purposes of the enterprise.

18. STRENGTH ALWAYS COMMUNICATES
Spirit

Elizabeth cultivated the appearance of an ethereal virgin, a combination of the Holy Virgin and the renaissance ideal of the pallid fair maiden. But she was no shrinking violet. From girlhood she had a passion for hunting and at age fifteen personally slit the throat of a fallen buck. Throughout her life, as one contemporary observed, she enjoyed killing "the great and fat stagge with her owen Hand." This was decidedly not usual for women in renaissance England, and Elizabeth's hunting companions were always men.

19. PROCLAIM YOUR DEVOTION
Dedication

On one occasion, Elizabeth declared that she would be pleased if her tombstone proclaimed "that a Queen, having reigned such a time, lived and died a virgin." With this, she pulled her coronation ring from her finger, held it up, and told her listeners that she would not wed, for she was "already bound unto a husband which is the Kingdom of England."

20. MAKE A SPECTACLE OF YOURSELF
Theater

It is no accident that William Shakespeare, Christopher Marlowe, and other playwrights, the greatest the English language has ever produced, rose during the so-called Elizabethan period. It was a time that embraced theater—not just on the stage but in all aspects of public life and religious ritual. Elizabeth relished the theater, both on the stage and in her own royal life. She eagerly participated in the public ceremonies preceding and surrounding her coronation. On the eve of the coronation itself, she made the traditional procession through the streets of London, pausing at every turn to respond to the many pageants and shows presented in her honor.

At one point, just before she mounted her chariot, Elizabeth turned to the people and loudly spoke a spontaneous prayer:

O Lord Almighty and Everlasting God, I give thee
most hearty thanks that thou hast been so merciful
unto me to spare me to behold this joyful day. And I
acknowledge that thou hast dealt as wonderfully and as
mercifully with me as thou didst with thy true and faithful
servant Daniel, thy prophet whom thou delivered out of
the den from the cruelty of the greedy and raging lions.
Even so was I overwhelmed and only by thee delivered.
To thee therefore only be thanks honor and praise forever.
Amen.

The allusion to Daniel was clever and effective indeed. To begin with, the story of Daniel in the lions' den was (as it remains) one of the most dramatic and popular biblical narratives. To Elizabeth's audience of common folk it was good, familiar theater. Even more important, of course, was the context of the story. Daniel had been thrown to the lions because he refused to deny the gift of prophecy given him and to forsake his tradition of prayer. The historical background of the biblical Book of Daniel was the tyrannical efforts of Antiochus IV to force the Jews of Palestine to abandon their religion and embrace pagan worship. Antiochus imposed increasingly brutal restrictions on the Jews, finally pillaging Jerusalem, and, in December 167 B.C., desecrating the Temple. This incited the Jewish rebellion that is described in the biblical Books of Maccabees.

Even the least educated among those who heard Elizabeth's prayer would have grasped the import of what she was saying: Like Daniel, she had been chosen by God to lead her people out of religious error. Like Daniel, she had been saved from the rapacity of the lions. By implication, Mary had been like Antiochus, a tyrant who had attempted to force a false religion on her people.

Theater is too often neglected by today's leaders. CEOs assume that their subordinates, their investors, and their clients want nothing more than hard numbers. The fact is that numbers are important; they appeal to the left brain, the logical side of all of us. But we are also driven by the right brain, the imagination, and to neglect that is to ignore half of human nature and human motivation. Elizabeth would prove herself a hard-headed businesswoman, intensely interested in tracking every shilling and penny her government spent. But she never sacrificed to this left-brain drive the appeal of imagination, of spectacle, of language vivified by strong image and metaphor. She never gave up her flair for theater.

21. BE A GREAT COMMUNICATOR
"Speech-making Came Naturally to Her"

Elizabeth was tutored by prominent classical scholars, most notably Roger Ascham, who held the office of public orator at Cambridge. In the renaissance scheme of education, knowledge and expression were much more closely identified with each other than they are now. To be educated was to be eloquent, and to be eloquent was to reveal a high degree of education. That Elizabeth was a brilliant student goes hand in hand with the judgment of one prominent modern historian of the period, Maria Perry, who declared that "speech-making came naturally to" Elizabeth who "quickly developed this talent with such style and flamboyance that contemporary annalists treasured even her most casual sayings."

Although few business schools seriously teach "eloquence," effective leadership is still largely a matter of communication. Indeed, immersed in our media-saturated sea, with sound bites continually floating, swimming, darting, and sinking around us, communication skills are more valuable than ever. How difficult it is in these noisy days to utter speech that is remembered for an hour, let alone is "treasured." An effective leader thinks about what he says, carefully crafting each utterance of any significance.

22. LESS IS MORE
A Simple Elegance

Although Elizabeth devoted far more time and attention to substance than to image, she hardly skimped on the latter. Her image was important to her because she understood it was important to those whom she led. Elizabeth did not hesitate to invest in costly gowns and jewelry; nevertheless, she always favored elegant understatement in her appearance. Her tutor, Roger Ascham, remarked of the young Lady Elizabeth, "She greatly prefers a simple elegance to show and splendour, despising the outward adorning of plaiting the hair and wearing of gold."

23. A LEADER IS NEVER CRUSHED UNDER THE WEIGHT OF A GRUDGE

Bygones

Students of Elizabeth's life and reign have sometimes wondered why the queen, once she had ascended the throne, made no attempt to rehabilitate the official status of her mother, Anne Boleyn. Anne, of course, had been executed on the authority of Henry VIII as an adulterous traitor, with the added result that Elizabeth had been formally declared a bastard. Upon ascending the throne, Elizabeth's half-sister, Mary I, acted almost immediately to declare the annulled marriage of Henry VIII and her mother, Catherine of Aragon, valid. But Elizabeth did no such thing to serve the memory of Anne Boleyn.

Why not?

To begin with, Anne Boleyn had been executed when Elizabeth was just over two and a half years old, so emotionally she probably meant little to the queen. The infant Elizabeth hardly knew her. More important, however, is that Queen Elizabeth realized the danger inherent in resurrecting the past. She did not want to call into question the actions of her father, lest she inadvertently offer ammunition to the opponents of his decision to break with the Roman Catholic Church. Nor did she wish to revive any of the controversy that had surrounded Anne Boleyn and her marriage to Henry. Elizabeth recognized that Anne was never popular with the people, and she had no desire now to defend the former queen or to remind the people that Anne, denounced as a traitor and the "whore of Babylon," was her mother.

An effective leader realizes that sometimes it is best to put aside personal feelings and let bygones be bygones. A leader's eye should be fixed on the present and the future, which offer both perils and possibilities, rather than on the past, about which nothing meaningful can be done.

24. MAKE A STRONG IMPRESSION
Suck It Up

Feeling weak? Feeling tired? A trifle down? You don't have time to look for some secret source of strength and rejuvenation. Just stop whining, take a deep breath, and fake it. People depend on you—and they are *watching* you.

Consider Elizabeth, who lived to seventy—an advanced age in a time when any woman was fortunate if she survived into what we would deem her middle years. The Queen exercised vigorously, relishing in particular dancing and the hunt, and she took care to broadcast an impression of abounding vigor and good health. Appearances, however, could be deceiving. Despite the vigor she exhibited, Elizabeth was frequently unwell and sometimes seriously ill. Nevertheless, in all but the most dire circumstances, she refused to yield to her various ailments. Even as she grew old, she chose not to slow down. She faced the fact that a leader must project strength every day, every moment, and in every contact with the outside world. This was especially important, she believed, for a woman leader, since powerful men the world over were waiting and watching for the least sign of her weakness.

Elizabeth, accordingly, cultivated habits of patient and courageous endurance. She never complained. She never magnified minor indispositions. In 1577, for example, suffering from a bothersome leg ulcer, she expressed an interest in taking the healing waters at Buxton spa. Lord Burghley, Elizabeth's long-serving adviser and confidant, thoughtfully sent her a flask of Buxton water, but she refused to touch it because (according to Burghley) "somebody told her there was some bruit of it about, as though her Majesty had had some sore leg." At times her efforts at concealment were amusing. Courtier Robert Cecil wrote to a friend in 1597: "The Queen hath a desperate ache in her right thumb, but will not be known of it, nor the gout it *cannot* be, nor *dare* not be."

Given the grim state of medicine in Elizabeth's day, hiding or even ignoring illness may well have been a sufferer's healthiest course of action. These days, however, no responsible manager or leader can afford to neglect his health, and it is no longer a good idea to ignore illness or even the suspicion of illness. But we also live during a time in which any number of management gurus advise us to loosen up, to let down our guard, to let those around us know that we, like them, are "vulnerable" (a favorite word of these writers).

Don't even *think* about following such advice.

Even today, Elizabeth would have none of the touchy-feely crowd, and neither should anyone who aspires to leadership. Your subordinates, your colleagues, and your bosses—*none* of them want to see you as weak, ailing, whining, complaining, or *vulnerable*. They want to feel and see strength and self-confidence, and you should oblige them by projecting these qualities.

This does not mean that you should avoid asking others for help or support when you need it. Knowing when you need the contribution and collaboration of others is hardly a sign of weakness; in fact, it is the mark of an effective leader and manager. Nor should you attempt to deceive yourself into thinking that you are invulnerable, immune to anxiety, fatigue, doubt, and, yes, illness. Take care of yourself. But also keep it to yourself—at least where the world of work is concerned.

25. STAY IN SHAPE
Fit for Leadership

Leadership is not of the mind alone. It is, in great part, a matter of physical presence, of creating a continually powerful *living* impression.

Elizabeth, fair-skinned, with reddish blond hair, beautiful in her apparent frailty, was enchanting as a young woman. In 1597, however, at the age of sixty-four, in an era when the average life span barely extended into early middle age, Elizabeth was still fit, vigorous, and agile. Calling on her that year, the French ambassador remarked how impressive it was "to see how lively she is in body and mind, and nimble in every thing she does." Another foreign visitor to the court during the fall of 1602, the year before her death, saw her out for a stroll, "walking as freely as if she had been only eighteen years old."

Her physical fitness was in part her good fortune, but it was also the product of rigorous exercise, especially hunting and dancing. Elizabeth treasured a lifelong reputation as a magnificent dancer. In February 1600, she allowed herself to be lured onto the floor at the invitation of a cousin of the queen of France who had come for a visit. One canny observer noted that the queen made the effort to entertain her visitor "to shew that she is not so old as some would have her." Two years later she partnered the French duke of Nevers when he came to England on a diplomatic mission. Her secretary of state, Sir Robert Cecil, later confided that she had not so much enjoyed the dance as she had danced to be courteous to her visitor. In observing "points of courtesy . . . to strangers," Cecil declared "she is no prince's second."

In old age, Elizabeth retained so much vigor that James VI, king of Scotland and prime candidate to succeed her to the throne of England, began to believe (presumably to his chagrin) that Elizabeth would "endure as long as the sun and moon."

Elizabeth did not deceive herself into believing that she could remain a girl forever, but she worked hard to forestall decay of mind *and* body. Moreover, she understood that the effective leader must be willing to demonstrate—not defiantly, but always gracefully—the health and vigor associated with young strength and the inspiring strength of ever-youthful hope, ambition, and pride.

26. TAKE THE PRESSURE OFF
Thinking on Her Feet

The ability to think fast, to express oneself cogently, and to retain one's composure under the pressure of the moment is indispensable to a leader. For that very reason, most of us put such a high premium on this quality that, in a given situation, we tend to demand from ourselves an even faster and better response than our questioner does. If there is pressure in the moment, we typically apply most of it ourselves. The result may be stammering incoherence or a hasty answer regretted in leisure.

Elizabeth, renowned for her quick wit and instant grasp of complex situations, practiced a useful tactic for avoiding overly hasty responses. One day during the closing decade of her reign, the French ambassador, André Hurault, Sieur de Maisse, called on the queen. He later reported that their conversation frequently strayed from the subject he had raised. Elizabeth repeatedly apologized for her digressions.

"See what it is to have to do with old women such as I am!" she self-deprecatingly exclaimed.

But the ambassador soon came to realize that these detours were not the meanderings of an aging mind but a deliberate tactic to buy more time to think through whatever issue the two were discussing. In this way, giving herself the time she needed to think effectively on her feet, Elizabeth relieved the pressure of the moment rather than added to it herself.

The result was brilliant conversation and shrewd negotiation. As the French ambassador admiringly remarked, "One can say nothing to her on which she will not make some apt comment. . . . She is a very great princess who knows everything."

27. A LEADER IS A LEADER IN EVERYTHING SHE DOES

Always as a Queen

Elizabeth was a great walker who habitually took her exercise in the form of a brisk walk around the grounds of Hampton Court. It was soon noticed, however, that she walked "briskly when alone," but that when she was conscious of being watched, "she, who was the very image of majesty and magnificence, went slowly and marched with leisure."

A leader is a leader in everything she does.

"... Be ye ensured that I will be as good unto you as ever Queen was unto her people. No will in me can lack, neither do I trust shall there lack any power. And persuade yourselves that for the safety and quietness of you all I will not spare if need be to spend my blood."

—ELIZABETH,
address on coronation eve

Three

"UNTO HER PEOPLE"

COMBINING THE COMMON TOUCH WITH
THE AIR OF LEADERSHIP

T*HOUGH A "VIRGIN QUEEN," ELIZABETH WAS NEITHER AIRY nor aloof. She combined an image of august majesty with a warm, common touch that created an instant and unbreakable bond with courtier and commoner alike. This chapter looks at how the queen reached out to embrace the people she led.*

28. YOU'RE IN A PEOPLE BUSINESS
It's About People, Not Policy

On December 30, 1548, the sixteen-year-old Elizabeth sent her brother, Edward VI, a New Year's present. It was her own translation of *Sermon on the Nature of Christ*, by the Italian monk Bernardino Ochino, who had visited England the year before. What she had chosen to translate and to present as a

65

gift was a sermon extraordinary for its straightforward sim-
plicity and directness in a time when complex sermons, full of
convoluted theology, were highly favored. Elizabeth, you may
recall, was the daughter of the king who had broken with the
Roman church. She grew up in a world and a nation torn by
religious disputation, in which learned men argued and dis-
coursed over Scripture as if they were lawyers verbally arm
wrestling over some gnarled legal brief, and in which thousands were slaughtered over seemingly trivial differences in
the practice of worship.

The gist of the sermon Elizabeth chose to translate is
this: Love Christ, and live by faith. Christ did not come to
give laws, but to bring grace. If Moses wrote on stone tablets,
Christ wrote on the heart. Most boldly, Ochino declared "that
Christ is the only mediator between us and the Father and
that we have no need for the invocation of saints. All that the
saints had was in Christ. . . . He came not just to purge
Sodom and Gomorrah with real fire, but to fill the whole
world with divine fire."

Christianity was central to the age of Elizabeth, but one
does not have to be a Christian or even religious to appreciate the message of the girl's gift to her brother. It is a message
of faith and love, to be sure, but it is also a message of humanity's taking precedence over any law or doctrine. While
church officials and monarchs argued and warred, Elizabeth
put herself on the side of what one of her biographers, Maria
Perry, calls "Christ's universal humanity." For her this was the

message of religious faith, which both underlay and transcended all the fine points of church law and doctrine.

Saint Paul, in his Second Epistle (Corinthians 3:6), wrote: "Not of the letter, but of the spirit: for the letter killeth, but the spirit giveth life." A teenager, Elizabeth already understood that the spirit—of religious faith, of political relationships, of the law—was far more important than the letter of religion, of government, of law. She understood what any number of pallid corporate functionaries down the ages and even today often fail to understand when they respond to the request of a customer, a colleague, or a subordinate with the phrase, "Well, that's against company policy." Policy is important, just as the letter of the law or the written word of religion is important. But effective leaders never seek to take refuge in these, to hide from people, or to evade their questions, requests, and needs. Effective leaders put issues of "universal humanity" ahead of blind obedience to rules, regulations, and prescribed procedure. They put people before policy.

29. ACKNOWLEDGE EVERYONE
Thanks

By October 1558, it was clear to everyone at court that Queen Mary I was seriously ill and, most likely, mortally ill. As it became apparent that Elizabeth would, after all, ascend the throne, courtiers and others deluged the twenty-six-year-old with offers of help and support. Elizabeth took the time to answer the onslaught of correspondence even if it was only with a note of thanks. Most of these were dictated to a secretary. One, dated October 28, 1558, is obviously the draft of a note written by a secretary. Elizabeth had taken pains to add a special closing in her own hand: "Your very loving friend Elizabeth."

Throughout her long reign, Elizabeth would never forget to thank and reward those who had done or offered her service. Nor, even as reigning queen, would she ever lose the personal, ever-humanizing touch suggested by her addition to this scrap of paper from 1558. Much of Elizabeth's success as a leader was her ability to project her humanity at all times. Certainly, this quality remains the basis of our continued interest in the queen. Over more than four hundred years she still comes across as a living, breathing, feeling person whose humanity seems more sharply delineated than many more recent—and even still living—leaders in politics and in business.

30. NEVER FORGET TO BE HUMAN
Words of a Child

During her precoronation procession through London, Elizabeth was greeted at Fenchurch by a child whose assigned task it was to welcome the new queen on behalf of the entire city. The tumult of the crowd, however, drowned out the child's words. Dramatically, Elizabeth called for silence, then listened attentively as the little girl recited her verse greeting. Eyewitnesses remarked the queen's "perpetual attentiveness" and a "marvelous change of look as the child's words touched her person."

Elizabeth never allowed herself to become so rapt in the loftiness of her station that she forgot to be human. Like all effective leaders, she remained connected to a root reality that gave her an unwavering perspective on whatever changing circumstances and challenges confronted her.

31. PLEDGE 100 PERCENT
Promise

To the lord mayor and people of London, Elizabeth, on the eve of her coronation, made this pledge:

> *And whereas your request is that I should continue your good lady and Queen, be ye ensured that I will be as good unto you as ever Queen was unto her people. No will in me can lack, neither do I trust shall there lack any power. And persuade yourselves that for the safety and quietness of you all I will not spare if need be to spend my blood. God thank you all.*

In short, Elizabeth promised to give to those she was called upon to lead 100 percent. To them she pledged her very life.

In the corporate world, few of us are required to lay down our physical lives, but it is essential that those we manage, work with, and lead be persuaded that our lives are indeed fully engaged with their individual needs and aspirations as well as with the organization as a collective whole. This should be the promise that underlies any leadership role.

32. BESTOW A SMILE
"A Most Smiling Countenance"

At the conclusion of the religious service following her coronation, Elizabeth walked from Westminster Abbey to Westminster Hall, bearing her orb and scepter, and, as one witness noted, "with a most smiling countenance for everyone."

If the occasion required, Elizabeth could present an awe-inspiring, even quite terrifying, demeanor to the world. It was said, for example, that she once soundly rebuked the commissioners she had dispatched to negotiate a treaty with France. She was so harsh, it was reported, that two of the commissioners swore they would carry her words "to their graves," and one of their colleagues begged the queen "to make them men again, who remain so amazed [stunned] as . . . nothing can breed any comfort in them." Yet Elizabeth was also well aware of the power of a smile to communicate confidence, trust, warmth, and approval, and she used this far more than her powerful faculties of criticism and rebuke.

33. WORK THE CROWD
Don't Be Shy

Elizabeth loved to work a crowd. She was a born actress who willingly made large and dramatic gestures to drive home a point or to create a bond between her and the people. At one ceremony, for example, near the beginning of her reign, a child (allegorically representing Truth) handed her an English Bible. The queen eagerly accepted it, kissed it, clutched it to her breast, and declared her promise "to be a diligent reader thereof." The crowd roared its approval.

Elizabeth's feeling for the masses made a dramatic contrast with the demeanor of her predecessor, Mary I, who was naturally shy and avoided contact with crowds. As a leader, Mary was, of course, a disaster.

Shyness may be forgiven and even cherished in personal friends, but it does not go down well in public life. In this arena, shyness is interpreted as aloofness, snobbishness, haughtiness, or even disdain of and disregard for the people. As a general rule, the most effective leaders are the most freely demonstrative, willing to make personal contact at every opportunity.

34. STAND UP FOR THOSE YOU LEAD
"They Are My People"

To a deputation of judges who came to pay their respects to the newly crowned queen, Elizabeth commanded: "Have a care over my people. . . . They are my people. Every man oppresseth them and [de]spoileth them without mercy. They cannot revenge their quarrel nor help themselves. See unto them, see unto them, for they are my charge."

In the last analysis, leadership is selflessness. It is a complete identification with and advocacy of the people one leads. Their well-being must be the foundation of the leader's well-being. The fates of leader and led must be one and the same.

35. ALWAYS CONSIDER
THE MIDDLE COURSE
Moderation

Shortly after she ascended the throne, certain Protestant zealots went about stripping the country's churches of the trappings of Roman Catholicism, including altars (which were replaced by communion tables), paintings (which were whitewashed out of existence), statuary (which were smashed or burned), and so on. Elizabeth acted quickly to stem the tide of this iconoclasm, decrying, for example, the destruction of the much-loved Cheapside Cross, which she called an "ancient ensign of Christianity." Although she was committed to enforcing the break with the Catholic Church, the queen also understood that the people would greatly resent the destruction of images and other objects that had grown familiar and comforting. She had no wish to alienate any of her subjects, and while she insisted that her senior clerics enforce uniformity of Protestant worship, she ordered a halt to the wholesale destruction of the traditional trappings of the country's churches.

Leadership often requires making unpopular decisions, but a skilled leader is also sympathetic to the feelings of others and takes care to avoid unduly upsetting or alienating anyone. This requires maturity, restraint, and the exercise of imagination and good judgment.

36. GET DOWN TO THE FRONT LINES
Out Among Them

Travel was no pleasure in Elizabethan England. Travel by sea was, of course, arduous and supremely hazardous, but even overland journeys within England were slow, tedious, filthy, and generally uncomfortable. They were also expensive. When Elizabeth and her court traveled overland, no fewer than four hundred wagons were required, together with as many as 2,400 packhorses, which moved along at a rate of perhaps twelve miles a day—on a *good* day. Two officials had charge of major court travel, the lord chamberlain and the lord steward. The chamberlain oversaw the small army of attendants attached to the Queen's Privy Chamber and also ensured that ceremonies were conducted properly and that the queen's safety was attended to. The steward ran the domestic departments, supervised the Keeper of the Queen's Jewels, and a host of clerks, cashiers, and accountants. He managed about a thousand people.

Why would Elizabeth go to the expense and the discomfort of these formidable expeditions—called "progresses"—virtually every summer?

"We come," she explained to the people of one town she visited, "for the hearts and allegiance of our subjects."

It is difficult to lead an enterprise by remote control, but it is all too easy to become a remote leader, cut off from the nitty-gritty realities of the enterprise. Elizabeth was determined that this would not happen in her case. Inconvenient, expensive, and even dangerous as it was, she saw to it that each summer the court made a progress through the land. What better way to communicate her affection, regard, and care for her people than by direct contact? What better way to cement the loyalty of her subjects than by direct contact? Moreover, what better way to assess the state of the nation than by direct contact with it?

During World War II, the American general George S. Patton, Jr., ordered all of his senior commanders to spend part of every day in the field, not behind a desk. It was important, Patton said, for a leader to be seen by his men, and it was also important for a leader to see for himself the situation of his forces. The same held true for Elizabeth, and the same holds true for any manager or executive. There is no substitute for frequent contact with reality in all its complexity and fullness—for seeing and for being seen—even if it takes a good deal of effort to "get out among them."

37. CREATE SATISFACTION
Of Human Bonding

During the summer of 1564, Elizabeth and her court embarked on one of their customary "progresses," a royal tour of the country to make contact with the people. On August 5, the queen arrived in Cambridge. She addressed the university there, speaking extemporaneously in beautiful Latin. She began:

> *Although that womanly shamefacedness, most celebrated university and most faithful subjects, might well determine me from delivering this my unlaboured speech and oration before so great an assembly of the learned, yet the intercession of my nobles and my own good will towards the university have prevailed with me to say something. And I am persuaded to the thing by two motives; the first is the increase of good letters, which I much desire and with the most earnest wish pray for; the other is as I hear all your expectations.*

The speech was a masterpiece of bonding. To begin with, Elizabeth presented herself with disarming humility, which was entirely appropriate to her audience. For, in Elizabeth's day, the university was an exclusively male dominion into which no woman, not even a queen, would boldly venture. The speech recognized this. Next, Elizabeth went on to flatter and elevate her audience, "so great an assembly of the learned." She then explained that, despite these things, which should discourage her from addressing the university, her "nobles" prevailed on her to speak and, even more important, her "own good will towards the university" persuaded her. In no uncertain terms, Elizabeth communicated her enthusiastic support for the enterprise of this audience. Moreover, she incorporated that enterprise into her plan for the entire realm: a desire for "the increase of good letters" (that is, higher learning). Thus, she not only communicated her high regard and support for the university, but also let her audience know that she believed they and their institution were performing a profoundly important national service. Finally, she concluded by telling her listeners that she was compelled to speak also by a desire to "hear all your expectations." Elizabeth wanted to hear what those learned people expected from her. The greatest honor a leader can bestow on those she leads is to give them a voice by inquiring into their wishes, needs, and wants.

But perhaps the most important leadership lesson to be learned from Elizabeth's address to the scholars of Cambridge is that she made the effort quite literally to speak their language, addressing them in learned Latin. The effect, according to eyewitnesses, was that the audience was "marvellously astonished" and roared their love and approval: *"Vivat Regina!"*

An effective leader learns the language of those she leads. In a business context, this may well be the language of business—that is, a language that speaks of dollars, value, time, rewards, risks. Whatever the organization, the leader must speak in a language that reflects its values, needs, and concerns. This often requires a certain selflessness, a humility similar to that with which Elizabeth approached her Cambridge audience. The focus must be removed from the leader's needs and wants and shifted to the needs and wants of the organization and its people. In this way, a distinctly human bond may be forged, a bond between leader and led that makes solid business sense.

38. DON'T BE BLINDSIDED
Grass Is Greener

Elizabeth loved England and the people of England, but she did not let her warm feelings cloud her cold, hard judgment. She spoke of the "inconstancy of the people of England" and of "how they ever mislike the present government and have their eyes fixed upon that person who is next to succeed." Elizabeth was identifying a characteristic peculiar not so much to the English but to human nature generally. In any organization, the powers that be typically face a similar situation: a tendency to find fault with the current leadership and to assume that the grass is greener elsewhere. For this reason a leader must remain responsive to the needs and wishes of the people he leads and must establish and maintain a bond of common interest with them. To the extent that people feel that they have a stake in the current leadership, they tend to be committed to that leadership and not to some hoped-for greener pasture.

39. GIVE A LITTLE, GET A LITTLE MORE
Quid pro Quo

In Elizabeth's England, the wealth of the great noble families was in decline relative to the rise in the wealth of the middle class, the class of merchants and entrepreneurs. For the sake of the English economy, Elizabeth wanted to foster the expansion and prosperity of the middle class, but she knew full well that she also needed the support of the old families, which were still influential and powerful. Toward this end, she developed a system of quid pro quo that was as elaborate as it was informal. She gave some important men extra time to repay their debts. She allowed them to remain generally undertaxed. Some she granted royal allowances, or she deeded to them certain royal properties. Beyond this, she showed a great interest in their family affairs and stood godmother to a welter of noble infants, well more than a hundred in all. In return for these services and considerations, Elizabeth expected support and loyalty. For the most part, she received both.

Sooner or later, most leaders learn to operate with the aid of informal quid pro quos. They create a kind of corporate karma, a network of relationships that facilitates business. For all her officially sanctioned power and authority, Elizabeth devoted particular effort to building her unofficial and informal network.

40. DO THE RIGHT THING
"Honour and Conscience"

After the Northern Rebellion of the late 1560s—a Catholic-led uprising in the north of England—Parliament continually pressed Elizabeth to order the execution of Mary, Queen of Scots, who was being held in the north country. Elizabeth refused, pointing out that Mary had originally come to England seeking refuge: "Can I put to death the bird that, to escape the pursuit of the hawk, has fled to my feet for protection? Honour and conscience forbid!"

It is not that Elizabeth was tender-hearted but that she had a strong sense of the rightness of things, of honor, and of conscience. Furthermore, she assumed that her people shared this very sense with her. If, Elizabeth reasoned, she acted contrary to her conscience, then surely her subjects would likewise perceive that she had done wrong.

Much of what Elizabeth did and said was guided by her profound religious beliefs, for religion permeated all aspects of sixteenth-century life far more than it generally does today. Yet, for the queen, morality and ethics were also based on an act of imagination, the ability to project her own moral sense onto the collective moral sense of her subjects. Based on this imaginative leap, Elizabeth resolved to commit no conscious wrong.

41. HAVE A GOOD TIME
The Queen's Men

Elizabeth was broad-minded and forward-looking. To the consternation of the Puritans who incessantly preached against public entertainment of any sort, the queen encouraged dancing and music, and she fostered the theater, including the work of an up-and-coming playwright named William Shakespeare. Elizabeth personally sponsored an acting troupe, known as the Queen's Men. She was also an enthusiastic fan of sports of all kinds, ranging from Sunday afternoon rowing on the Thames to bearbaiting, a blood sport in which a chained bear was set upon by hounds in an enclosed arena. As the famed nineteenth-century historian

Thomas Macaulay observed, the Puritans objected to bear-baiting not because it was cruel to the bear, but because it gave pleasure to the people.

Elizabeth never confused order and religious observation with the absence of pleasure. She believed in recreation and the refreshment of spirit, and she encouraged these things among her subjects. As for herself, she once risked scandalizing the more conservative members of her court by declaring, "I like silk stockings well. They are pleasant, fine, and delicate. Henceforth I will wear no more cloth stockings."

42. SHOW YOUR CONCERN
Care

In 1572, Elizabeth made her customary summer "progress," a royal journey through many parts of her realm for the express purpose of making contact with her subjects. At Warwick Castle she was treated to a mock battle and a spectacular fireworks display. As it turned out, the display was rather *too* spectacular. It set fire to some houses in the nearby town of Gorhambury, completely destroying the home of an elderly couple.

Accidents will happen, and Elizabeth was not obliged to make any manner of restitution to the people who had suffered damage, Nevertheless, she saw to it that her courtiers ponied up £25 12s. 8d., more than sufficient for the elderly couple to rebuild their house and furnish it as well. The queen was also demonstrative in expressing her sympathy for the pair and her thankful relief that they had not been harmed. All of this made sufficient impression on the locals and on Elizabeth's entourage to have been preserved by history for some 450 years. A leader should never forget that few acts of care, concern, and kindness are so small as to escape notice. On such momentary acts, enduring reputations are built.

43. SHARE THE DANGER
"To Live or Die Amongst You All"

At Tilbury camp on the eve of an anticipated invasion by soldiers of the Spanish Armada, Elizabeth, wearing the body armor of a cavalry officer, spoke to her troops:

> *My loving people, we have been persuaded by some that are careful of our safety to take heed how we commit our self to armed multitudes for fear of treachery, but I assure you, I do not desire to live to distrust my faithful and loving people.*

Given the instability of England on the verge of invasion, many feared that Catholic sympathizers would aid the Spanish by attempting to assassinate the queen. Some of the queen's advisers told her that it was folly to walk exposed among armed men. The danger was real, but Elizabeth believed that the greater danger lay in seeming to neglect her duty, to fail to make personal contact with the defenders of her realm. She decided that it was critically important for her to share their dangers and, by so doing, to lift their spirits and inspire victory. In addressing the troops, however, she did not trumpet her courage or her sense of duty but, rather, her absolute trust in them, her "faithful and loving people." She continued:

> *Let tyrants fear, I have always so behaved myself that under God I have placed my chiefest strength and safeguard in the loyal hearts and good will of my subjects. And therefore I am come amongst you as you see at this time not for my recreation and disport, but being resolved in the midst and heat of the battle to live or die amongst you all. To lay down for God and for my kingdom and for my people my honour and my blood even in the dust.*

Too often the rank and file feel little if any bond with those who manage or lead them. If the project fails, the workers will be laid off, the supervisor fired, the manager demoted, but the CEO, at the worst, will float gently to earth on his golden parachute. Elizabeth made certain that no one in *her* audience would see things this way. I am "resolved . . . to live or die amongst you," she says, powerfully and unmistakably communicating that *she* will share *their* fate.

Then she continues, doing now what all leaders of true genius do. After identifying herself absolutely with her subordinates—her subjects, her soldiers—she lifts herself above them. She is, after all, their leader.

I know I have the body of a weak and feeble woman but I have the heart and stomach of a King, and of a King of England too, and think foul scorn that Parma or Spain or any Prince of Europe should dare invade the borders of my Realm to which rather than any dishonour shall grow by me, I myself will take up arms, I myself will be your General, Judge, and Rewarder of every one of your virtues in the field. I know already for your forwardness you have deserved rewards and crowns and we do assure you in the word of a Prince, they shall be duly paid you.

There are no lofty abstractions in this motivational speech. Instead, Elizabeth identifies herself as a leader whose ferocity is more than equal to the occasion. She has not only the heart of a king, but the stomach of one, too—and not just of any king, but a king of England. She asserts personal command of the situation. And then she really levels with her men. Where other monarchs, princes, presidents, and commanders would speak of the glory of battle and the honor of doing one's duty, Elizabeth speaks of more tangible rewards. The performance of each man, she says, she will view as a "Judge" and will duly reward the same. What greater motivation than to assure those you lead that, first, they have already performed well, and, second, their continued excellent performance will be noted, appreciated, and rewarded?

Now, Elizabeth knew that she was neither Joan of Arc nor an Amazon warrior princess. She was a woman of fifty-five. And while she would serve, in spirit, as "General, Judge, and Rewarder":

> *In the meantime my Lieutenant-General shall be in my stead, than whom never Prince commanded a more Noble or worthy subject, not doubting but by your obedience to my General, by your Concord in the Camp and your valour in the field we shall shortly have a famous victory over those enemies of God, my Kingdom and of my People.*

Elizabeth endorses and empowers her designated commander, who serves in her stead. These, the closing words of her speech, not only are a vote of confidence for the man assigned the task of leading the defense of England, but they directly deputize him so that there can be no mistaking the degree and depth of his authority.

A leader must choose his deputies wisely and then must treat them as true deputies, leaders in their own right who enjoy the full support and confidence of the chief—who, indeed, stand in for that chief. There can be no doubt of this confidence and this authority. There can be nothing said to dilute it. The sense created among the rank and file must be of the full empowerment of their immediate leaders. The more transparently these leaders stand between them and the chief, the more committed and efficient everyone will be.

44. SPEAK FLUENT BODY LANGUAGE
To Win the Hearts of the People

One of Elizabeth's subjects conveyed this observation on the way the young queen worked a crowd:

> *If ever any person had either the gift or the style to win the hearts of the people, it was this Queen. All her faculties were in motion, and every motion seemed a well-guided action; her eye was set upon one, her ear listened to another, her judgment ran upon a third, to a fourth she addressed her speech.*

Elizabeth was a "people person" whose charisma, by all accounts, was extraordinary. Was this quality a gift of the gods? For some leaders—"born leaders," we call them—it is. But take another look at the insightful description above, penned by an onlooker more than four centuries ago. The skills the queen exhibited can be learned, honed, and perfected by anyone.

- She uses and coordinates her body language thoughtfully so that "every motion" seems a "well-guided action." (Another witness spoke of the "perpetual attentiveness in her face.")

- She conveys the impression that everyone with whom she comes in contact is important to her.
- She makes and maintains eye contact with the people she meets and greets.
- She listens to people—and shows that she is listening.
- She pays attention to people.
- She talks *with* and *to*—not *at*—people.

Of such skills—none supernatural—is effective leadership built.

*"Some think [one] thing,
some [an]other; whose judgement
is best God knows."*

—ELIZABETH,
*on differences between the Catholic
and Anglican communion service*

Four

KEEPING THE FAITH

CREATING COMMON CAUSE WITHOUT TYRANNY

M UCH OF A LEADER'S TASK IS TO KEEP EVERYONE ON THE *same page—without forcing everyone to say the same words or sing the same notes. The organization must move in a single direction, but never in lockstep. Elizabeth guided her nation to uniformity of religious worship—and, thereby, uniformity of national identity—yet without coercing a single conscience or compromising the individual mind, heart, and imagination.*

45. PUT FIRST THINGS FIRST
Setting Priorities

As has been made clear in the prologue to this book, the England that Elizabeth was called on to lead was deeply troubled. Crowned and enthroned, the young woman faced a potentially overwhelming set of problems. But she did not allow herself to be overwhelmed. Instead, she set priorities.

She saw as the two most immediate problems her relations with Spain and France, the most powerful nations in Europe, and the question of her role in the church, specifically the issue of royal supremacy, the doctrine whereby the head of the English state was also the head of the Church of England.

As far as relations with Spain were concerned, Philip II, widowed husband of Mary I, had already proposed marriage to Elizabeth. Such a union would ensure peace and alliance with Spain, but at the cost of sacrificing the Protestant Reformation in England (Philip was Catholic) and at the cost of diluting British sovereignty by union with the son of the Holy Roman emperor. The majority of the English people favored Protestantism, Elizabeth knew, and she had no desire to compromise British nationalism. Yet, at this point in time, England was engaged in intense peace negotiations with France. If the French learned that relations between Spain and England had deteriorated, the French negotiators would begin to treat England as a weakened and vulnerable power. Elizabeth, therefore, dared not offend Philip II by rejecting him outright. She resolved to hold Philip at a cordial arm's length until negotiations with France had been concluded.

In the meantime, she turned to the issue of royal supremacy. Many faithful Englishmen were concerned by Saint Paul's pronouncement that no woman could be an apostle, shepherd, doctor, or preacher. How, therefore, could a woman be supreme head of a Christian church? At this time

English bishops still had a voice among the Christian churches of Europe. It was feared that if England now went against the teachings of Saint Paul by nominating Elizabeth head of the nation's church, the bishops would lose all power and influence in Europe and, indeed, would fight hopelessly among themselves.

Elizabeth assigned the resolution of this dilemma to a class of professionals about whom she often voiced mistrust and distaste: the lawyers. They did away with the phrase "Supreme Head of the Church" and substituted "Supreme Governor of the Church." This was sufficient to gain passage in Parliament, on March 18, 1559, of a bill abolishing papal supremacy and establishing royal supremacy. Elizabeth was now unquestioned "governor" of the Church of England.

In the meantime, she received the news that peace had at last been concluded among England, Spain, and France by the Treaty of Câteau Cambrésis.

Elizabeth knew all too well that nothing is permanent. Religious dissension might well resurface and the peace might well prove fragile, but for the present her top two priorities had been successfully dealt with. Now, and only now, she turned her attention to the important details of religious observance and began to take steps to institute uniformity of ritual, particularly in the celebration of Mass, throughout English churches.

Ritual was of great importance in the age of Elizabeth when the vast majority of the population was illiterate and came to know governing authority chiefly through the church, and came to know the church almost exclusively through its rituals. Thus, through the details of worship were conveyed the message of the individual's place in the world and in the nation. Enforcing uniformity of religious worship, Elizabeth understood, would be to create uniformity of government and the universal acceptance of her authority. But she also understood that the edifice of ritual required a firm foundation in the form of peace among nations and the assurance of her role as supreme authority in church matters. Surely it must have been tempting to begin her reign by issuing decrees dictating the forms of worship, but such decrees, without foundation, would have been impossible to enforce. If a royal decree could not be enforced, royal authority would amount to little more than empty formalities. So she held issues of religious uniformity in abeyance until the more basic issues of peace and supremacy had been resolved.

In the unnerving onrush of events, it is little wonder that many managers and CEOs feel themselves overwhelmed. There is a strong drive to leap into the fray and do *something*. This impulse is natural, instinctive, but often wasteful and even destructive. Analysis of priorities may not appear to the world like action, but it is action nevertheless, action that conserves precious resources and multiplies their effectiveness by ensuring that one step is appropriately built on another. Perhaps it was the long, difficult childhood and youth of Elizabeth that developed in her a coolness of judgment enabling the panic-free analysis of priorities. However she came by this trait, it served her throughout her reign as an essential component of leadership.

46. COMMUNICATE DIRECTLY AND OFTEN
"Through So Many Ears"

Elizabeth remarked to Parliament on a basic problem of communication: "Do I see God's most sacred word and text of holy writ drawn to so diverse senses be it never so precisely taught and shall I hope that my speech can pass forth through so many ears without mistaking, where so many ripe and diverse wits do oftener bend to construe, than to attain the true and perfect understanding?"

If the word of God Himself may be so variously interpreted and wildly distorted, Elizabeth complained, what hope does she, a mere mortal, have that her words, passing "through so many ears," will be interpreted with "true and perfect understanding"? Under the best of circumstances, Elizabeth implies, distortion of meaning will take place. In the case of her meaning, which is broadcast to any number of disputatious and competing politicians and religious leaders, it is bound to be bent utterly out of shape; for many of the queen's hearers would rather "bend" her words "to construe" a meaning to suit their particular agenda than to "attain the true and perfect understanding" of those words.

Elizabeth articulated a problem that all leaders encounter. Through imprecision of language, imperfection of human understanding, and ulterior motives to deliberately distort, what one says is not always interpreted as one intends it to be. Those with responsibility for leadership must be fully aware of this fact of life and must, accordingly, begin by speaking with great precision and clarity. Beyond that, they must monitor the response to their speech and be prepared to correct honest misinterpretation and counter deliberate distortions. It is also important to communicate as directly as possible, rather than at second or third hand. Everyone has seen how rumors take on lives of their own as they are passed from one person to another and then to another and so on. Each interpreter adds his own spin or imparts his own biases. Prevent this by communicating directly—and often.

47. TO EVERYTHING THERE IS A SEASON
Timing Is Everything

Elizabeth saw to it that her half-sister, Mary I, was buried, on December 14, 1558, with full Catholic rites. She could have signaled the return of Anglican Protestantism by denying the dead queen such a burial. But she knew that Mary would have wanted to be buried as she had lived, a Catholic, and Elizabeth honored that. Even more important, she had no wish to raise the obvious divisive religious issues before her own coronation had taken place. A more rigid ruler—Mary herself, for example—would have insisted on publicly enforcing the new rituals. Under Mary, however, England had been drifting swiftly toward religiously based civil war. Elizabeth's own convictions urged her to steer England back to Protestant practice, but her political instincts told her that timing is everything. The corpse of the queen was not a fit field on which to fight a battle between two faiths. Just as she had been willing to adopt the outward show of Catholic worship during the reign of Mary, in order to preserve her life, Elizabeth was now willing to give Mary her last Catholic rites in order to preserve the peace of the nation. She had time, and she would take no sudden, rash, rigid actions.

Many leaders adhere absolutely to absolute principles and the letter of the law or the company policy book. They will tell you that such a course is a hard course but a necessary one.

In reality, such a course is an easy course. Too easy.

To adhere rigidly to a set of principles is to ignore, deny, or defy the nature of any human business, which is always tied to time, to people, and to events. Time, people, and events change, engender change, and demand change; absolute adherence to principle allows for no change. Principles, rules, laws, policy: For the effective leader, these are important guides. But their application always takes place in time and is therefore subject to timing. Elizabeth, a deeply religious woman, regarded Anglican Protestantism as an absolute good—and thus timeless—but she also understood that it was her task to apply it in the changing context of human government, a context very much dependent on time. She consequently compelled herself to be sufficiently flexible to bide her time.

Those who lead must apply any absolute with extreme care and judgment, admitting, accepting, and understanding that principles and precepts are absolute while people and circumstances are relative. The timing of rules and policies, their introduction and enforcement, is critical. Forcing the issue typically produces resentment, suspicion, anxiety, and even catastrophe.

48. ACTING FOR THE LONG TERM
A Matter of Principle

There were many in Elizabeth's government who criticized the queen for not having married the husband of her late half-sister, Mary I. A union with Philip II would have continued the alliance with Spain, which some of Elizabeth's advisers believed was vital to the well-being of England. Elizabeth responded to this criticism in her 1572 speech to Parliament:

> *If policy had been preferred before truth, would I, trow [think] you, even at the first beginning of my rule have turned upside down so great affairs or entered into tossing of the great waves and billows of the world that might, if I had sought my ease, have harboured and cast anchor in most seeming security? It cannot be denied but worldly wisdom rather bade me knit and match myself in league and fast alliance with great princes to purchase friends on every side by worldly means.*

In short, "policy"—that is, political expedience—dictated that Elizabeth should have married Philip II to perpetuate the alliance with Spain, thereby *purchasing* "friends on every side by worldly means."

So why didn't Elizabeth do it? Why didn't she take the course of smooth expedience rather than enter into "tossing of the great waves and billows of the world"? She explains:

All these means of leagues, alliances and foreign strengths, I quite forsook and gave myself to seek for truth without respect, reposing my chief stay in God's most mighty grace.

Rather than take the easy way, the expedient course, Elizabeth chose the path of "truth"—truth "without respect," by which she specifically means without regard for negative consequences to the alliance with Spain. The "truth" she chose was to found a genuinely Protestant state, rather than continue what her half-sister had begun, the undoing of the Protestant Reformation in England. Marriage to the Catholic Philip II and a consequent bond with Spain would have meant that England would be a Roman Catholic country.

All of this is historical fact, and it is certainly highly relevant to the history of England, which under Elizabeth not only maintained its Protestant identity, but, in doing so, remained free of entangling alliances. The rewards of this freedom outweighed the considerable risks involved. Although England often had to stand alone, it could also operate with great scope and freedom in a world that, during the sixteenth and seventeenth centuries, was expanding as mariners from England (and elsewhere) pushed west to the continents that would come to be called the Americas.

Beyond the historical significance of Elizabeth's decision to pursue the path of "truth" rather than "policy" is a more general lesson for leaders. It is about balancing expedience against principle, about taking aim at the "truth"—however that may be defined in a particular case—and not allowing oneself to be turned from that course. If the "truth"—one's ultimate goals and aims and principles—is wisely chosen, the rewards are far more enduring and substantial than what mere expedience offers.

> *Thus I began* [Elizabeth continued her speech], *thus did I proceed, and thus I hope to end. These seventeen years God hath prospered and protected you with good success under my direction, and I doubt not but the same maintaining hand will guide you still and bring you to ripeness and perfection. Consider yourselves the bitter storms and perils of your neighbours . . .*

49. RESPONDING TO CHALLENGE
The Nature of Command

By the standards of her day, Elizabeth was a monarch tolerant of nonconforming religion. This is not to say that she advocated freedom of religion as we understand it today, but the actions of her half-sister, Mary I—"Bloody Mary"—who authorized the burning of hundreds of Protestants, or of Catherine de Médicis, who authorized and perhaps even planned the massacre of thousands of Huguenots, were far more typical of Elizabethan-era monarchs than the policies and actions of Elizabeth. Nevertheless, Elizabeth judged it critically important to end in England the religious strife that threatened to tear her realm apart. One way she saw to do this was to enforce uniformity of worship. The Anglican Church prescribed ritual precisely. Roman Catholic practice differed from this prescription, of course, but so did the more extreme form of English Protestantism known as Puritanism. When Elizabeth learned that Puritans in several English counties were conducting so-called prophesyings—essentially prayer meetings—in defiance of Anglican uniformity, she wanted them stopped.

Elizabeth did not order any violent repressive action but instead, in 1574, directed Archbishop Matthew Parker to suppress the prophesyings. Parker had not succeeded in this commission by 1576 when he died, and in December of that year, Elizabeth summoned to her presence his successor, Edmund Grindal. She told him that she wanted these meetings stopped. Grindal replied that he could not find it in his heart and conscience to condemn them. Furthermore, in a written "remonstrance" to her, Grindal pointed out the limits of Elizabeth's authority in ecclesiastical matters and exhorted the queen to respect the authority of bishops. Elizabeth, as supreme governor of the Church of England, immediately suspended Archbishop Grindal from exercising his "metropolitan functions"—that is, his authority over the provincial clergy.

To a greater degree than most rulers of her age, Elizabeth was typically motivated by moderation and a spirit of compromise. But like any leader who wishes to establish and preserve effectiveness, she knew decisively where to draw the line. In the matter of uniformity, there could be no compromise. The concept of *uniform* worship was, of course, fundamentally incompatible with the essence of compromise. Uniformity is prescriptive, a black-white, either-or, yes-no issue. In the absence of absolute compliance from her immediate subordinate in this matter, Elizabeth curtailed the archbishop's authority.

The dispute with Grindal would drag on until his death in 1583, and, of course, Elizabeth did not succeed in eliminating Puritanism from England. It would continue to take root, spread, and, in 1642, result in the Great Civil War led by the Puritan Oliver Cromwell. Depending on how one wishes to view history, this outcome may be seen as evidence of the futility of Elizabeth's actions to enforce uniformity or as a vindication of them. After all, she was right. Without uniformity, the country was torn apart, and the monarchy even came to an end for an extended period with the overthrow and execution of the hapless King Charles I.

The lesson for leadership here is a most difficult one, especially in today's management climate. Essentially, it is this: Each leader must decide to what degree he can afford to allow his leadership to be challenged. When is it appropriate to bend, to compromise with challengers? And when is it necessary to control them, to limit them, and even to fire them?

These days, most managers and executives go to great lengths before they reprimand or transfer, let alone fire, a "challenging" subordinate. Often, some combination of personal inclination and company policy and legal or quasi-legal constraints conspire to discourage or even prevent jettisoning the Archbishop Grindals of the corporate world. Personnel decisions are difficult, especially when challenges to authority are involved. However they are attended to, they *must* be attended to rather than ignored in the hope that they will just go away. And somewhere, at least in the mind of the manager, the executive, or the CEO, a line must be drawn defining the limit of flexibility and compromise.

50. CREATING COMMON CAUSE
Consensus Maker

In contrast to her father, Henry VIII, Elizabeth steered clear of theological debate. This prompted some to accuse her of knowing little of "divinity," to which she tersely replied that she had "studied nothing but divinity till I came to the crown." Her avoidance of theological matters had nothing to do with lack of knowledge or lack of interest; it was a desire to suppress any matter that might fuel religious dispute among the senior clerics, thereby imperiling the religious consensus she was struggling to achieve. She made the objective of this consensus crystal clear, dismissing an argument on the fine points of theology by declaring that "there was only one Jesus Christ, and one faith, and all the rest they disputed about [are] but trifles."

Consensus-building leaders must emphasize the areas of agreement rather than those of disagreement. Part of doing this involves showing how the areas of agreement vastly outweigh areas in dispute. It is an issue of focus and proportion. If this means suppressing some aspects of the subject at hand, it is a judgment call that the leader must be willing to make.

51. GETTING YOUR PEOPLE IN LINE
"Breach of Unity"

To an assembly of senior clerics of the Church of England, Elizabeth complained about their laxity in enforcing uniformity of Anglican practice and in suppressing Puritanism:

> *You suffer [allow] many ministers to preach what they list*
> *[like] and to minister the sacrament according to their*
> *fancies [whims], some one way, some another to the*
> *breach of unity. Yea, and some of them are so curious in*
> *searching matters above their capacity as they preach they*

wot [know] not what—that there is no Hell, but a
torment of conscience. Nay, I have heard there be six
preachers in one diocese the which do preach six sundry
[different] ways. I wish such men to be brought to
conformity and unity.

Elizabeth had a temper, which many men did fear; however, her more usual way of expressing displeasure with a given situation was to lay out the problem, then call for a course of action. That is, her purpose was not to intimidate those she led but to manage and motivate them. She did this by choosing to focus not on personal deficiencies or failings but on the problem at hand and on what might be done to address the problem.

In the case of religious uniformity, the problem was that the bishops, whom she addressed, permitted "many ministers to preach what they list." This was a failure of management, for the job of the senior clergy was to interpret doctrine and see to it that the subordinate clergy, the parish priests, preached in uniform accordance with that doctrine. As Elizabeth saw it, her senior managers were not adequately doing their principal job, which was to create and maintain uniformity of worship.

After leveling her criticism of the bishops, Elizabeth continued by developing specific examples of the problem. Note her use of the word "fancies"—referring to the imagination or whim. These nonconforming preachers, she claimed, were not preaching out of profound conviction but out of mere imagination and whim. Furthermore, some preached "one way, some another"; it was not even a case of organized dissent. After pointing out that these errant preachers were simply out of their depth ("searching matters above their capacity" and preaching "they wot not what"), Elizabeth cited a specific example of spectacular error: "that there is no Hell, but a torment of conscience." With this single example, Elizabeth demonstrated that what was at issue was not a few fine points of ritual, theology, or interpretation, but major pillars of religion. It was "such men," the queen said, that are "to be brought to conformity and unity."

This brief passage is a valuable example of how a very good manager goes about obtaining the results she wants. There is no browbeating, no name-calling, no shouting. Instead, there is a straightforward exposition of a current deficiency, an explanation of the consequences of that deficiency, and a specific, dramatic example of it. By way of conclusion, the queen made unmistakably clear what she wanted: "I wish such men to be brought to conformity and unity." No threats were made, nor were any required. For the consequences of failing to carry out her wishes—the consequences of failure to enforce "conformity and unity"—were abundantly clear from the explanation and example Elizabeth provided. This is the ideal method for motivating subordinates to execute a management policy: no external threats but a firm understanding of the *natural* and *inevitable* consequences of failure. To achieve this level of motivation, the manager must, like Elizabeth, clearly define

the problem, explain it, illustrate it, then issue straightforward orders that cannot be misinterpreted.

52. RECOGNIZING LIMITS
Realism

To promote the creation of uniform worship throughout the
land, Elizabeth called for the placement of qualified, learned
clergy in every parish. In the queen's day, the very purpose of
a university education was almost exclusively to educate the
clergy—and it was an expensive proposition. The Archbishop
of Canterbury pointed out to the queen that there were thirteen thousand parishes in England, of which only one in
twenty could afford to pay a minister the £30 per year thought
necessary to meet minimum living expenses. Fully two thousand parishes could ante up no more than £8 per annum.
Hearing this, Elizabeth exclaimed: "Thirteen thousand! It is
not to be looked for!"

Faced with the reality of the situation, Elizabeth
responded realistically. If not all her clergy could be fully educated, at least they could be chosen to meet a tolerable minimum standard as "honest, sober and wise men, and such as
can read the scriptures and homilies well unto the people."

Ignoring reality will not make it go away. A major part of
the job of an effective leader is to look for creative ways to
meet reality at least halfway.

53. STOP QUIBBLING
Conviction

A leader never ignores the details and the technicalities but always sees beyond them, ensuring that the spirit of a value or a belief is given more weight than its mere letter. Thus, dotting the i's and crossing the t's never becomes more important than the meaning of the message itself. Even as a young woman (Elizabeth's biographer Christopher Hibbert observed), the future queen's religious "faith was sincere but it was not, nor ever was to be, darkened by prejudice or bound by dogma: she had no interest in the pettifogging quibbles with which her father concerned himself."

54. TO TELL THE TRUTH
"As Lawyers Do"

Few professions are looked on with more suspicion and doubt than the practice of law. "How do you know when a lawyer is lying?" begins a familiar joke. "His lips are moving."

This distrust is hardly peculiar to our time. The foremost Elizabethan playwright, William Shakespeare, allows a butcher in his *King Henry VI, Part 2* to fantasize on his idea of utopia: "The first thing we do," the character says, "let's kill all the lawyers." Elizabeth, too, objected to approaching the truth in the manner of a lawyer, twisting, and turning, deliberately distorting, and looking for loopholes. The matter of revealed religion, as she saw it, was a simple case of absolute truth, yet: "I see many overbold with God Almighty making too many subtle scannings of His blessed will, as lawyers do with human testaments."

Many events and issues, especially in business, are open to wide interpretation and debate. But it is up to each person involved in an enterprise, and in particular to the leaders of the enterprise, to identify certain core truths from which policy and action must not vary. These principles should be presented, understood, and acted upon without ambiguity or the "subtle scannings" of lawyers and those who would behave like lawyers, seeking to bend principle to suit expedience. Without such firmness, an organization rests on shifting sand.

55. TAKING THE PATH OF CREATIVE COMPROMISE
"Whose Judgement Is Best God Knows"

Elizabeth wanted to reinforce national unity by enforcing uniformity of religious worship, yet she did so while still allowing considerable latitude. For example, the Bill of Uniformity she supported prescribed the use of a prayer book approved in 1552; however, to make the prayer book more palatable to conservative, Catholic-leaning clergy, Elizabeth allowed the addition of a sentence from a 1549 prayer book. This sentence, which implied that Christ was literally present in spirit in the communion service—essentially a Roman Catholic position—was set alongside a sentence from the 1552 prayer book, which conveyed the Protestant notion of the strictly symbolic nature of the communion service. It was a compromise. As Elizabeth later remarked to a Scots diplomat: "In the sacrament of the altar, some think [one] thing, some [an]other; whose judgement is best God knows."

Moderation is often a more successful path to achieving one's goals than an unyielding insistence on a single doctrine. Yield what can be yielded to achieve what you absolutely want to achieve.

56. CREATING COMPLIANCE WITHOUT KILLING CONSCIENCE
Uniformity and Conscience

Elizabeth was hardly a liberal leader, but neither was she a tyrant. In the matter of religious worship, for example, she believed that outward conformity to the state religion—uniformity in the practice of worship—was essential to creating and maintaining a national identity. She would not budge on this point, and she endorsed legislation that outlawed non-Anglican forms of public worship, both Catholic and Puritan. Yet she drew the line at instituting anything resembling a

Spanish Inquisition. While she firmly believed that it was her right and her duty to enforce uniformity of outward practice, she did not believe that she was entitled to pry into the conscience of the individual. It was a case of demanding that her subjects render unto Caesar only that which is rightly Caesar's. What they privately believed, however, was a spiritual matter beyond the proper reach of the state. Many historians have attributed the general prosperity, the economic growth, and the cultural flowering of Elizabethan England to the queen's commitment to freedom of conscience.

A leader or manager can expect and demand certain levels of performance and conformity, but this does not extend to control of the individual heart, soul, mind, and imagination. To be sure, a skilled leader will appeal to the "inner person," but he must stop short of any coercion or compulsion.

57. GIVING THE WORD AND TAKING THE LEAD
A Leader Leads

From our twenty-first-century perspective as citizens of a great democracy, it is not always easy to sympathize with the leadership views of Queen Elizabeth I. Schoolbook history, for example, paints the seventeenth-century New England colonist Anne Hutchinson (1591–1643) as a kind of heroine of American democracy before there even was an

American democracy. Recall that Anne was banished from the Puritan Massachusetts Bay colony in 1637 because she dared to voice her belief in individual perception and conscience, not the word of Bible and priests, as the source of religious truth.

We honor her for that, but Elizabeth—had she known of her—would have condemned her utterly and absolutely. Here's what the queen said about religious self-inspiration and self-direction: "I must pronounce [this] dangerous to a kingly rule," the queen told Parliament, "to have every man according to his own censure, to make a doom of a validity and privity of his Prince's government with a common veil and cover of God's word, whose follower must not be judged, but by private men's exposition."

This Elizabethan mouthful requires translation. It is this: Allowing each person to make his own judgment of the validity of "his Prince's government" is dangerous to central authority—to "kingly rule." Indeed, Elizabeth concludes, "God defend you from such a ruler that so evil will guide you." Pray to the Lord that you never have a king who allows everyone to be his own ruler!

We don't have to reject more than two centuries of our own democracy to accept an important part of the truth Elizabeth opens to us. The chief point is this: If you are going to lead, lead. Decide in what areas you want input from others, including discussion and debate, but decide as well just where your word must be law. Then hold to this and make no apology for it. It is your responsibility. Relinquishing your authority to popular opinion may seem the right thing to do, and people will like you for it—at first. But sooner or later the organization will drift and falter. When this comes to pass, you'll find yourself without the absolute authority to change course but with exclusive possession of all the blame for the course into which your hapless enterprise has wandered.

Without counsel plans go wrong,
But with many advisers
they succeed.

—*Proverbs 15:22*

Five

GOOD COUNSEL

Building a Loyal Staff—and a Loyal Opposition

P OPULAR MYTHOLOGY, ESPECIALLY AS PURVEYED BY
Hollywood, has often portrayed Elizabeth as contrary and
headstrong, a difficult woman heedless of counsel. The fact is that
Elizabeth devoted a great deal of time and effort to staffing her
Privy Council and meeting with that body. She appreciated
expertise and never hesitated to consult experts on matters of great
moment. Few leaders have been better served by their advisers
than Elizabeth—but, then, few leaders have ever been so careful
to acquire such good counsel.

58. FORGIVE, BUT DON'T FORGET
Anger and Revenge

With the death of her half-sister, Mary, Elizabeth became
queen of England. But for much of her young life she had

been subject to emotional torture, suspended between grace and disgrace, power and powerlessness, and even life and death. Count Feria, Philip II's trusted diplomat from Spain, counseled the new queen to avoid displaying a desire for revenge or anger.

It is interesting advice. Feria did not counsel her to shun anger or revenge but to avoid *displaying* a desire for these things. His assumption, of course, was that Elizabeth must yearn to vent her rage in vengeance. It's only natural.

But Elizabeth stunned Feria by replying that all she wanted was to make those who had wronged her, the councillors who had accused her of plotting against Mary, *admit* that they had wronged her. Once they had done this, her intention was to pardon them. Elizabeth, as if by instinct, understood what the seasoned Spanish diplomat apparently did not understand: that vengeance creates a cycle of vengeance in return, that ill treatment breeds ill treatment in return, that rule by fear destroys all opportunity to create loyalty.

Yet if Elizabeth wanted to forgive, she was not willing to forget. It was important to her that she begin her reign with the air cleared. It was not necessary to purge *people*, but it was critically important to purge misunderstanding and any sense that wrongdoing had passed unnoticed. Elizabeth wanted to know where she stood, and, equally important, she wanted those around her to know that *she* knew where *they* stood— or, in any case, *had* stood. None of this was for the purpose of vengeance, but, rather, for the sake of information. A leader needs to know the people he leads.

And there was more. By pardoning the wrongdoers, Elizabeth could create a bond of loyalty, or at least gratitude, even as she asserted power over those she pardoned. Forgiveness, thoughtfully applied, is among a leader's most powerful and persuasive resources.

59. BEWARE OF RADICAL CHANGE
Continuity

After Elizabeth's ascension to the throne, Sir Nicholas Throckmorton, one of her advisers, cautioned that she could "succeed happily through a discreet beginning" and that she should bear a "good eye that there be no innovations, no tumults or breach of orders." The new queen took such advice to heart. She retained the most capable members of the Privy Council, dropping only those whose Catholicism was unbending and who were solely committed to the policies of "Bloody Mary." Even so, she retained a number of Roman Catholic councillors, for she had no desire to create alarm among the people or to suggest that a new reign of persecution was about to begin.

In general, evolutionary change is preferable to revolutionary change. Elizabeth sought to preserve the best of what had come before her, but without allowing continuity to block necessary and desirable change.

60. FAVOR EVOLUTION OVER REVOLUTION
New Blood

From the outset, at the very first meeting with her Privy Council following the death of Mary I, Elizabeth informed the current members that she would "shortly appoint . . . others meet for my service," new council members, for the "aid" of the current members and "for ease of their burden." There could be no question that Elizabeth was within her rights to appoint to the council whomever she chose. But instead of high-handedly bringing the new people in, she took pains to consider the current members when she made her announcement. Not only would new blood serve *her*, she said, but it would also aid the present council by easing the burden of all members.

There is a natural tendency among new leaders to shake things up, to act out that old saying about a new broom sweeping clean. More skilled or seasoned leaders realize, however, that few organizations are so rotten that they require a thorough sweeping. The effective leader cherishes what is best in an existing organization while simultaneously transfusing new life into it. The introduction of new blood into any organization can be an intimidating, even threatening process. Most leaders acknowledge this, but very few do anything to ease the introduction of fresh faces and new minds. The underlying attitude is like it or lump it.

And such an attitude is well within the leader's rights. But that doesn't make it an effective or desirable leadership strategy. People who feel threatened not only begin to make poor decisions, but also generate deep resentments. Their unhappiness soon permeates the organization, to the detriment of all. The lesson here? Have a care for your present human assets when you introduce new ones.

61. SEEK THE WISDOM OF OTHERS
"Good Advice and Counsel"

"I mean to direct all mine actions by good advice and counsel," Elizabeth announced to her Privy Council at her first meeting with them on November 20, 1558, three days after the death of Mary I. The new queen believed in the supreme importance of surrounding herself with wise, prudent, and competent advisers. She combined two broad categories of staff on her Privy Council:

1. The "ancient nobility": Elizabeth remarked to them that, "having your beginnings and estates of my progenitors, Kings of this realm," this category of adviser "ought in hon-

our to have the more natural care for the maintaining of my estate and this commonwealth."

2. Those "lately called": These newcomers had been appointed, Elizabeth said, in consideration and reward of their "service" to one of her predecessors, Edward VI or Mary I.

Although Elizabeth would add her own choices to the council as time went on, she recognized the value of retaining the best of the old order, for they represented continuity as well as faithfulness of long standing. They also had the greatest stake in the welfare of the Tudor government, having been given their place in the world by Elizabeth's "progenitors, Kings of this realm." Yet Elizabeth also believed that government is dynamic, and she valued the addition of advisers who recently proved themselves by actual service to the country.

From the beginning, an effective leader devotes much thought to his immediate subordinates, his inner circle. Ideally (and this is how Elizabeth saw it), this staff would blend elements of continuity with new blood, the skills and energy of people who have only recently proven themselves. To this base the new leader adds his own most trusted staff members. Elizabeth did not make the mistake of simply "firing" the council she had inherited. Instead, she subjected her inner circle to a gradual leavening process, continually blending the old with the new, the staff she inherited with personnel of her own choosing. In this way, continuity was assured, yet stagnation was avoided. In this way, too, Elizabeth crafted a loyal staff, yet one that did not consist of clones of herself or like-minded yes-men.

62. MAKE EXPECTATIONS CLEAR AND LOFTY
I Give You This Charge

Queen Mary I died on November 17, 1558. After the prescribed three days of mourning, Elizabeth summoned the Privy Council and other nobles to the Great Hall of her estate at Hatfield. She addressed the assembly, beginning this way:

> *I give you this charge, that you shall be of my Privy Council and content yourself to take pains for me and my realm. This judgement I have of you that you will not be corrupted with any manner of gift and that you will be faithful to the State, and that without respect of my private will, you will give me that counsel that you think best; and, if you shall know anything necessary to be declared to me of secrecy, you shall show it to myself only and assure yourself I will not fail to keep taciturnity therein. And therefore herewith I charge you.*

Many, perhaps most, managers who fail begin by failing to make their expectations crystal clear. Elizabeth issued her "charge" with the clarity of a diamond. There can be no mistaking the mission she lays down for the members of her Privy Council:

1. To give 100 percent, not only for "me," but for "my realm."

2. To remain uncorrupted. Note that the queen begins by declaring that she believes her council to be uncorrupted and incorruptible. Her expectation is that she will not be disappointed in this belief.

3. To serve the State faithfully.

4. To be frank—even at the risk of giving personal offense. No boss begins by declaring that what she wants is a team of "yes-men," and many bosses ask for frankness, enjoining the team members to "pull no punches" or to "tell it like it is." Yet how many bosses really mean this? That is, when one of the team members questions a judgment call, how many bosses can avoid responding defensively or with anger? If you ask for frankness, be prepared to accept and to reward it, no matter how personally unsettling it may be. If you ask for straight shooting only to dodge the bullets angrily, what ultimately bites the dust is your credibility.

5. To share secrets confidently. This is a most delicate "charge." The leader who invites confidence must take care never to violate that confidence. Assuring your subordinates that their secrets are safe with you is far more a "charge" to yourself than it is to them, for it can be very difficult to "keep taciturnity therein."

63. REQUIRE LOYALTY
"To Require of You All Nothing More but Faithful Hearts"

Elizabeth was renowned for frank speech to those who served her. Today, we would call her a straight shooter. At her first meeting with her Privy Council, on November 20, 1558, she told the members that she meant to "require of you all nothing more but faithful hearts, in such service as from time to time shall be in your powers towards the preservation of me and this commonwealth."

The first requisite of an effective leader is to communicate all expectations with unmistakable clarity. Thus, Elizabeth began with her chief expectation: the maintenance among her staff of "faithful hearts." It is a richly meaningful phrase, combining loyalty with honesty—loyalty to the leader as well as to the organization ("this commonwealth") and honesty, including honesty to oneself. In emphasizing that she required "nothing more but faithful hearts," Elizabeth communicated her expectation that each member of her staff would operate always as his own man, in accordance with his own true feelings, albeit for the "preservation of me and this commonwealth." She asked, that is, for *unselfish* faithfulness to self.

A true leader never demands unthinking obedience or loyalty. This can be had better from machines than from human beings. The purpose of a staff of managers and advisers is to extend the effective vision of the chief executive officer, not simply to augment his nearsightedness or intensify his blindness. Only a staff of independent thinkers can enable the

CEO to see far beyond the walls of his office, provided that these independent thinkers have "faithful hearts" in the fullest sense of that phrase as Elizabeth intended it: faithfulness to themselves in greater service to the organization ("this commonwealth") and in personal loyalty to the CEO. As Elizabeth conceived it, a Privy Council exquisitely balanced the vital qualities of the faithful heart, which required nothing less than continually weighing self against others, the common good, and collective purposes.

64. EXCLUDE NO ONE
"They Which I Shall Not Appoint"

Too many organizations—whether governments or corporations—become crystallized, frozen into an inner circle hardened against an outer circle, divided into an insular, defensive core of decision makers versus everyone else. The results of such an organizational structure include, at best, a lot of wasted resources. The talent of the outer circle is rarely exploited productively. At worst, rigid enmities develop between the inner and outer circles. Instead of bonds of common purpose, there is resentment and distrust. Cut off from the sources of power, the outer circle may fall apart, its members becoming demotivated, simply drifting away or even actively banding together against the inner circle. In a government, revolution, civil war, or a coup may result. Analogous catastrophes, including various acts of passive aggression or even outright sabotage, may occur in a corporate context. At the very least, severely stratified corporations never achieve their full potential for productivity.

And yet there is value in cultivating an inner circle, a trusted band of advisers, large enough to afford a spectrum of opinion and judgment, yet small enough to manage, so that debates are never endless, and action is always possible.

Elizabeth cultivated her inner circle, the Privy Council, but she was careful not to alienate those who remained outside of this august group. In her speech to the first meeting of the Privy Council on November 20, 1558, a meeting that included nobles who were not yet on the council nor would ever be appointed to it, Elizabeth included the following remark: "And they which I shall not appoint [to the Privy Council], let them not think the same for any disability in them, but for that I consider a multitude doth make rather disorder and confusion than good counsel, and of my good will you shall not doubt, using yourselves as appertaineth to good and loving subjects." In other words, Elizabeth declared:

- A Privy Council should be small enough to be useful, to give "good counsel" rather than the "disorder and confusion" created by a "multitude"; therefore, only a few persons could be appointed to the Council.

- Failure to be appointed to the Privy Council does not signify being out of the loop: "of my good will you shall not doubt."

- None of you will be excluded from government, provided that you behave as "good and loving subjects."

Leadership requires choices—all the time, every day. Many of these choices require value judgments, including promotions, selections, appointments, and the like. Those promoted, selected, or appointed naturally feel good about it. Those passed over don't feel good about it. And that, too, is a natural response. An effective leader motivates the selectees without demotivating, let alone alienating, those who are not selected. This may be done as Elizabeth does here:

- by explaining the process of selection in some objective, relatively nonjudgmental way. In this case, Elizabeth emphasizes the necessity of keeping the Privy Council small.
- by persuading those *not selected* that they have not been *rejected.*
- by assuring those not selected that they still have the regard, respect, and confidence of the leader.
- by reaffirming the continuation of the "contract" between the leader and the subordinates, including those not selected. Elizabeth assures them of her continued "good will," provided that they behave as "good and loving subjects."

65. LEARN TO LEAN ON OTHERS
Sorting It All Out

Elizabeth developed a close working relationship with her extraordinarily able secretary of state, William Cecil, Lord

Burghley. One of the most valuable services he performed for her was the preparation of memos addressing major issues or problems facing the government. In these memos, Cecil would outline the problem and then, with great precision, list the various courses he believed available to the queen.

A leader does not simply *lead* others. She also works *with* others to formulate strategy and to make decisions. Elizabeth often spoke of her most trusted advisers as her "eyes." The people with whom you work should help you see more things and see them more clearly.

66. REWARD CONFIDENCE AND LOYALTY
"She Puts Great Store by the People Who Put Her in Her Present Position"

As Queen Mary I lay dying, her husband, Philip II, grew concerned about preserving the Anglo-Spanish alliance. He sent one of Spain's most adept diplomats, Count Feria, to sound out Elizabeth on this topic. After talking with her, Feria was shocked by the young woman's frankness and candor. He was also surprised that she "puts great store by the people who put her in her present position," valuing them above others—including Philip himself—regardless of their rank or political importance. Elizabeth was determined to build loyalty by rewarding loyalty. She would promote from the inside. It was a lesson in leadership this young, frail-looking woman offered to the sophisticated diplomat from Spain.

67. KNOW WHO IS WHO
AND WHO TO KNOW
"She Knows Who Is Who"

Count Don Gomez Feria, Spain's ambassador to England, remarked of Elizabeth shortly after she ascended the throne that "she knows who is who in the realm, at least among those of rank."

Elizabeth made it her business to know everyone of power, influence, and talent in her realm. And she did not rely on hearsay for this knowledge. She forged personal relationships with movers and shakers, drawing conclusions about what they could do for her and against her. Based on this knowledge, she guided the ship of state.

Subordinates are resources to the degree that they are well known. To the degree that they remain unknown quantities, they are potential threats and liabilities.

68. BE AN AVID READER OF PEOPLE
Judge of Character

Thomas Seymour, the dashing and ambitious lord high admiral, ultimately lost his head because he acted selfishly and impulsively. Although it is not likely that Elizabeth was actually in love with Seymour, as rumored, or that she had become in any way romantically involved with him, it is beyond question that she found him attractive, charming, appealing, and fascinating. Yet she was never seduced by him, either sexually or, what is more important, intellectually. When sentence was executed upon Seymour, Elizabeth is reported to have remarked coolly: "This day died a man with much wit and very little judgement."

Even as a very young woman, Elizabeth developed the habit of judging character clearly and objectively, separating superficial attractiveness from the deeper and more enduring qualities of mind and judgment. She also understood that one may be very smart and possessed of great wit, yet still lack sufficient judgment to keep one's head fastened to one's shoulders.

69. REWARD BOLDNESS BUT CHERISH JUDGMENT
Sir Walter

Everyone has heard the tale of Sir Walter Raleigh and how he spread his cloak across a mud puddle rather than let Elizabeth step into it. The story may even be true. Certainly, it is the kind of gallant gesture that would have appealed to a consummate courtier like Raleigh.

He was born in Devon about 1552, and as early as 1569 was fighting on behalf of the Huguenots (French Protestants) in the Wars of Religion in France. He subsequently attended college at Oxford (1572) and then studied law at the Middle Temple (1575). In 1580, he was off to fight the Irish rebels, and it was his frank and outspoken criticism of English policy in Ireland that brought him to the attention of Queen Elizabeth. She saw him as a problem solver, a doer, and a man of action. By 1582 he was chief among her court favorites. The queen rewarded him with monopolies, properties, and influential positions.

Yet, for all the responsibility she gave Raleigh, Elizabeth was not heedless of his boastful ways and his tendency toward extravagant spending. His enterprise had acquired for England a vast tract of the New World, a realm Elizabeth herself instructed Raleigh to call Virginia in honor of her status as the Virgin Queen. Nevertheless, Elizabeth concluded that, bold and brilliant as he was, Raleigh possessed inherently flawed judgment. Over the years, the queen continued to consult him and to support his New World ventures, but she conspicuously kept him off the Privy Council. He was too prideful, too contrary—in the words of one contemporary, "insolent, extremely heated, a man that desires to seem to be able to sway all men's fancies, all men's courses."

Elizabeth used the strengths of those around her while making allowances for their weaknesses. Always attracted to boldness, dash, and decisiveness, she was never seduced by these qualities—at least not for long. She used and rewarded Raleigh as far as she judged it safe to do. Beyond this point, she began to distance herself from him and to distance him from the main sources of power and influence.

Raleigh's fate, after Elizabeth's death, vindicated her wary judgment of him. His unremittingly aggressive policies toward Spain did not go down well with James I, who succeeded Elizabeth in 1603. As he became increasingly alienated from the king, Raleigh's tone turned more and more strident, giving his many enemies an ample opening to work his ruin. Before the end of 1603 the reckless Raleigh was accused of plotting to overthrow James. Convicted, the death sentence pronounced upon him was suspended, but he was imprisoned in the Tower of London until 1616 when he was released but not pardoned. With James's blessing, Raleigh financed his second expedition to Guyana in South America, pledging to find and operate a gold mine there that would realize great profit for England but not provoke renewed war with Spain. When no gold was found, King James reactivated the death sentence that had been suspended in 1603. Raleigh was executed in 1618.

70. HONOR YOUR HONORS BY BESTOWING THEM SPARINGLY
Largesse

One of the great prerogatives of a monarch—and, indeed, of many leaders—is the power to distribute rewards among subordinates. For Elizabeth, some of this largesse was directly financial, but often the rewards were of a more honorary nature, including knighthoods and peerages. To confer these cost her nothing, and so it was tempting to distribute them freely. Elizabeth realized, however, that to do so would create a kind of inflation that would soon reduce the value of the rewards. Therefore, she resolved to practice a policy that "honoured her honours by bestowing them sparingly." Elizabeth was notoriously parsimonious in the distribution of honors, a policy that served to magnify the value of each of them.

Managing people requires, among other things, managing incentives. Reluctance to distribute incentives erodes morale and diminishes performance; however, the indiscriminate distribution of incentives will do even greater violence to morale and will diminish performance all the more rapidly. As usual, the best course is a middle one.

71. PEOPLE: COLLECT THE BEST
"No One Could Escape Her Network"

One of Elizabeth's veteran courtiers advised an up-and-coming young man to "let nothing draw thee from the Court. Sit in every Council." Elizabeth's inner circle was the center of power in England, and success in the life of the court was a key to success in life, period. No one was more aware of this than Elizabeth herself, who set great store by good counsel and fully exploited all the power and prestige she could offer in order to secure such counsel. As her lord chancellor remarked, "The Queen did fish for men's souls, and she had so sweet a bait that no one could escape her network."

Leaders typically have plum jobs and power positions to offer deserving subordinates. These should not be distributed according to personal affection but according to ability. Gather closest to you the very best people whose loyalty, knowledge, and skill can be counted on.

72. YOU CAN'T PLEASE EVERYBODY
"The Insatiable Cupidity of Men"

The writer and courtier John Lyly tried in vain to obtain an important office from Elizabeth. "A thousand hopes," he wrote, "but all nothing; a hundred promises, but yet nothing." It wasn't that Lyly did not deserve the post but that Elizabeth had only so much largesse at her disposal, only so many "goodies" to dispense.

"No prince's revenue be so great that they are able to satisfy the insatiable cupidity of men," she once observed. It was a version of the lesson that parents have been teaching their children for time out of mind: *You can't please everybody.*

Yet it is a lesson that many leaders are unwilling to learn, a truth that they are unwilling to accept. The fact is—as Elizabeth well knew—the pie is always finite. Slice it too thin, and a great many will be displeased. Slice it too thick, and a great many will be displeased. Somewhere between these extremes lies excellence in management, and it is the wise manager who learns that such excellence has little to do with perfect bliss and universal happiness.

73. YOU HAVE MANY CONSTITUENCIES
"Nobles of Divers Humours"

As she approached the throne, Elizabeth understood and accepted that hers was a disordered realm and far from united. As she remarked to the French ambassador, she "had to deal with nobles of divers humours [temperaments]," and she was well aware that many of her subjects, "although they made great demonstrations of love towards her, nevertheless were fickle and inconstant." As the French ambassador recorded, "She had to fear everything."

Elizabeth never made the mistake of assuming that her subjects, whether advisers of state or people of the common street, thought as she did or felt as she felt. She saw that she had many constituencies to serve and could not, therefore, be single-minded or complacent but would have to be vigilant and flexible. A leader never takes unity and harmony for granted.

74. USING YOUR CARROTS
Redistributing Wealth

Many of the Anglican bishops during Elizabeth's time enjoyed ownership of rich "temporalities," large estates and other valuable properties. Elizabeth, looking for ways to build loyalty among the nobles and courtiers, yet faced with a royal treasury that, in the early years of her reign, was hardly over-flowing, put pressure on the bishops to rent their lands to select laymen at rates far below their market value. This was hard on the bishops, but it served Elizabeth's loyalty-building purposes—without so much as touching the treasury.

All leaders have some valuable commodities to distrib-ute—power, prestige, salaries, perks, whatever—and they must see to it that these are distributed in ways that build an organization and their own authority within the organization. Unfair, capricious, or careless distribution of the "goodies" creates dissension, discontent, a general demotivation, and, in the worst case, rebellion.

75. CONSTRUCTIVE CRITICISM
Faultfinding

Constructive criticism is part of a supervisor's or manager's job. It is an important aspect of program improvement as well as of individual mentoring. There is, however, a big difference between constructive criticism and faultfinding. The first addresses problems that can be corrected and even suggests solutions. It is criticism directed not at personalities but at problems, at issues. The second, in contrast, often attacks faults for the sake of the attack, without regard to the possibility of improvement. That is, the object of faultfinding is not remedy but criticism itself. Worse, faultfinding is generally directed at a person or at people rather than at issues and problems. If sales are off, the creative leader looks for ways to direct the attention of his staff to problems requiring solution. He does not tell his sales force that they don't know how to do their jobs or that they are bad salespeople.

Elizabeth was always ready with creative criticism, and she was unsparing with it; however, she drew the line at attacking personalities or private faults. "My own [faults]," she confessed to Parliament, "have weight enough for me to answer for." And she went on to suggest that each man and woman must answer for his or her own private faults, implying that no third party might answer for them or has the right to offer criticism of them.

76. REQUIRE EXCELLENCE
"If They Do Not Dance to Her Liking"

In 1597, a diplomat visiting Elizabeth's court observed that "when her maids dance she follows the cadence with her head, hand and foot. She rebukes them if they do not dance to her liking and without doubt she is mistress of the art."

Elizabeth was a demanding taskmaster, but her demands always came from personal knowledge of how a thing should be done. By demanding excellence she usually obtained excellence.

77. BE THE BOSS
"I Will Have Here One Mistress but No Master"

Of the suitors with whom Elizabeth was linked over the years, she was probably actually closest to Robert Dudley, Lord Leicester. Did Elizabeth love Leicester? Perhaps. By common consent he was a charismatic, highly attractive man. What is certain is that, for a number of years, he was the favorite of her court and was entrusted with a number of important duties and missions.

Yet whatever her personal feelings for Leicester, Elizabeth never forgot her authority. One day in 1565, Leicester argued with her because the queen refused one of his "men"—presumably, a servant—entrance to the Presence Chamber. Elizabeth put an end to the dispute by exclaiming with an oath, "God's death, my Lord, I will have here one mistress but no master."

In an age of absolute monarchy, when many rulers were nothing less than dictators who would brook no debate over their decisions, Elizabeth was remarkably liberal. Typically unafraid of disagreement, she invited debate on the most important questions. Yet she never let a doubt be created as to who held final authority. There would be but one mistress and no master.

A political friend of President Harry S Truman gave him a nameplate for his desk. It bore a motto that became closely identified with the thirty-third president of the United States: "The buck stops here." In this simple phrase, Truman summed up the essence of leadership, much as Elizabeth had done more than four centuries before: The leader willingly accepts both ultimate authority and ultimate responsibility. This may sound autocratic and even dictatorial, but, in fact, in a well-defined business context, it is a very liberating position. When all members of the enterprise understand and accept the final authority and responsibility of a designated supervisor, manager, executive, or CEO, they are freed up for action, secure in the knowledge of the source of authority for what they do and secure in the knowledge of a resource of appeal if something goes wrong. True leadership does not limit free-dom. It creates and enables freedom.

78. IT'S NOT A POPULARITY CONTEST
The Dilemma of Leadership

In a 1572 speech to Parliament, Elizabeth gave credit to God for the continuance of her reign. For without God's help, how could she have remained in power?

> *Can a Prince that of necessity must discontent a number to delight and please a few (because the greatest part are oft not best inclined) continue a long time without great offence, much mischief or common grudge?*

Elizabeth's answer to this rhetorical question is "No, no, my lords. . . . I attribute [my continued rule] to God alone. . . ."

How many supervisors, managers, and other leaders today find themselves wishing for some form of divine guid-ance, help, or intervention? Leadership can be a tremendous burden, especially if, as Elizabeth saw it, the leader must make many unpopular decisions, decisions that "discontent a num-ber to delight and please a few."

We live in a democracy based, in part, on a philosophy that most of us take for granted: that leadership decisions are made to discontent the *fewest* and to please the *most*. In Elizabeth's day, the idea of the greatest good for the greatest number, a philosophy that would come to be called Utilitarianism, didn't exist and would have been thought dangerously radical at best or, more likely, just plain nonsense. The sixteenth-century belief was as Elizabeth expressed it: that "the greatest part are not oft best inclined," that the things most people want are not best for the common good. For us in twenty-first-century America this is entirely unacceptable. Yet, in the context of business leadership, how many times have you heard (or have said yourself or have wanted to say) in defense of an unpopular *but necessary* decision: "Look, this company is *not* a democracy."

And, let's face it, most business organizations are not democracies and cannot be run as such. We may espouse various systems of participatory management, team structures, and flexible hierarchies, but when it comes down to it, managers are not elected by the employees they lead, and sometimes—maybe even often—managers and other business leaders must make unpopular decisions. They must be willing to "discontent a number."

Clearly, Elizabeth accepted the necessity of creating discontent. For most of us today this reality of leadership is harder to accept. But an effective leader must be willing to embrace this basic dilemma of leadership: that what the majority desires is not always or necessarily what is good for the enterprise. Moreover, each leader must be prepared to formulate strategies for dealing with this dilemma; that is, each leader must create an environment that allows him to make unpopular decisions and still remain viable as a leader.

Elizabeth's strategy was, in part, her conviction that she was guided by God and that she was—as all monarchs considered themselves to be—God's servant on earth. In part, too, Elizabeth cultivated a personal relationship with her people. She built loyalty in the people, a confidence in her good faith, which gave her the room she needed to make the political decisions she thought necessary without regard for their popularity or unpopularity.

It is important for the modern manager to accept the necessity of making unpopular, decidedly undemocratic decisions, at least from time to time. Yet it is equally important for the manager to separate those decisions from his relationship to his subordinates. That is, he must build among his subordinates confidence in the good faith behind his actions. Like Elizabeth, the effective business leader must create the room required for making *all* necessary decisions, including (and especially) the unpopular ones.

79. BE PREPARED TO GO TO THE MAT
Backing 100 Percent

In obedience to Elizabeth's policy of enforcing uniformity of religious worship throughout England, the Anglican bishops acted to suppress the Puritans and other "deviant" sects. When members of the House of Commons criticized these senior Church of England clergymen for their actions, Elizabeth assured the clerics of her full support: "We understand," she said, "that some of the Nether House [the House of Commons] have used divers speeches against you, tending greatly to your dishonour, which we will not suffer [tolerate]."

This single sentence is a wonderful example of how to convey 100 percent backing to people who, on your behalf or at your behest, have stuck their necks out. The first two words of the sentence are critical: "We understand." This is always a first step in sympathetic communication. All verbal exchange involves the risk of accidental misunderstanding or even willful failure to understand. A declaration of understanding—*we understand*—goes a long way toward assuring your listeners that *their* problems, needs, and wants will not meet with incomprehension or indifference.

Elizabeth went on to express her understanding that the bishops faced great pressure from some in the House of Commons. It is not enough to say that you understand, although this *is* a great deal; it is also necessary to explain your understanding. This offers proof of your sympathetic grasp of the situation and gives your listeners the opportunity to correct you if necessary. After all, it *is* possible that you do not fully understand the situation or that you in some way misunderstand it.

The queen concluded by assuring the bishops that she "will not suffer"—that is, not tolerate or allow—speeches directed against the honor of the clergy who act faithfully in her service.

Later in this speech to the clerics, Elizabeth very deliberately included herself among the targets of the criticism that was being hurled by people who claimed that the Church of

England had no clear doctrine of its own. This impression, the queen told her audience, had been created by toleration of nonconformist worship practices and ritual. "I pray you," Elizabeth enjoined the bishops, with reference to those who would vary from religious uniformity, "look unto such men." That is, watch out for nonconformists—and bring them into line.

Not only then did the queen express her understanding of the pressures operating on the bishops and her sympathy for their plight as well as her promise to support them against their detractors, but she ended the speech by telling them that she, too, had her critics in matters of religion. This created a common cause with the bishops. But Elizabeth went on to add a twist to her situation. Whereas the bishops had been subject to criticism for enforcing uniformity, the queen's problems were the result of incomplete, inadequate enforcement. This being the case, Elizabeth ended by asking her bishops for an even greater and more vigorous commitment to enforcing religious uniformity.

The great leaders are, first and foremost, great motivators. A mediocre leader would have addressed the bishops perhaps similarly to Elizabeth, but only up to a point. That is, she would have expressed understanding, sympathy, and support. But then such a leader would likely give in to a common, quite understandable, and even laudatory emotion. Likely, she would have apologized to the bishops for having directed them to actions that made their lives difficult.

But Elizabeth was no mediocre leader. Having expressed full understanding of and fellow feeling for the bishops' difficult position and having guaranteed them her support, she pressed them quite skillfully to pursue the unpopular policies of uniformity even *more* vigorously. That is, she asked them to step further into the hot water, to take even more heat.

Any competent manager can direct men and women who are already motivated to achieve. A great leader can do the same for those who are tired, discouraged, and fearful.

80. ALWAYS LAY IT ON THE LINE
Consequences

To ensure that the senior clergy of the Church of England would succeed in enforcing uniformity of worship throughout England, Elizabeth pledged to give them her full support. Should they fail in their duty through "negligence," however, Elizabeth made an equally unambiguous promise: "If you . . . do not amend [the "faults and negligence" of the church], I mean to depose you."

If you can't *do* the job, you'll *lose* the job.

An effective leader never makes idle threats, especially concerning demotion or termination. But an effective leader does lay it on the line: *The job needs to be done. Do it or someone else will.* Just as retaining a position and advancing in it are functions of success, losing the position is a function of failure—an inevitable consequence. While a leader should not browbeat, bully, or threaten, a leader should never hesitate to present consequences, both good and bad.

81. DELEGATE—THEN SUPPORT
Turf

Elizabeth delegated John Whitgift, the Archbishop of Canterbury, to enforce religious uniformity throughout England. When some in the House of Commons disputed with Whitgift, the queen intervened, sending a message to the Speaker that the Commons was not to "meddle with matters of the Church." To back this up, she vetoed all bills that encroached on church affairs.

Elizabeth had made an assignment and had established the turf of her delegatee; then she gave him the backing he needed to accomplish the mission she had assigned. A leader has the right to expect his subordinates to do hard things, but they, in turn, have a right to expect the leader's backing—and not just in the form of encouraging words but by vigorous, practical steps as well. The worst thing a leader can do is delegate an assignment and then fail to back the delegatee.

82. DON'T PLAY FAVORITES
Reining In

Elizabeth sent her trusted favorite, Robert Dudley, the earl of Leicester, to lead the British armies in the Netherlands. She gave him strict instructions, limiting the authority he was to assume in the Low Countries. However, shortly after he assumed command and without the queen's permission, he accepted the title of governor-general of the Netherlands.

Elizabeth was enraged on two counts: First, Leicester had usurped authority. Second, Elizabeth did not want to provoke Philip II of Spain unduly. It was a serious enough matter that she had chosen to intervene in the Netherlands. If she allowed her commander to assume the political title of governor-general, this would be a clear sign that she was acting directly against the government Philip had instituted. It would surely spark war. The queen sent a dispatch to Leicester:

> *How contemptuously we conceive ourself to have been used by you, you shall by this bearer understand, whom we have expressly sent unto you to charge you withal. We could never have imagined (had we not seen it fall out in experience) that a man raised up by ourself and extraordinarily favoured by us above any other subject in this land would have in so contemptible a sort broken our commandment, in a cause that so greatly toucheth us in honour, whereof although you have showed yourself to make but little accompt in so most undutiful sort, you may not think that we have so little care of the reparation thereof as we mind to pass so great a wrong in silence unredressed; and therefore our express pleasure and commandment is that all delays and excuses laid apart, you do presently upon the duty of your allegiance obey and fulfil whatsoever the bearer hereof shall direct you to do in our name whereof fail you not, as you will answer the contrary at your uttermost peril.*

Elizabeth expressed the reprimand in justifiably personal terms by letting Leicester know that she felt personally betrayed. Such a strategy of correction can work only in a context in which leadership is based, in large part, on a structure of personal loyalty. After expressing her sense of personal hurt, Elizabeth reminded Leicester in no uncertain terms of his duty to obey her, in effect his commander in chief.

Yet Elizabeth also understood that, in accepting the title of governor-general, Leicester had broken the egg. The situation could not be readily repaired in a way that would both appease Philip and avoid offending the Dutch, who had, after all, bestowed the title. The queen, as usual and despite her very personal outrage, settled on an intelligent, moderate, compromise course. She accepted that Leicester was her "lieutenant-general" but that, on Dutch soil, he might well be termed "governor-general." For his part, Leicester saw to it that in Utrecht when St. George's Day was celebrated, an empty throne was placed at the head of the banqueting table. Leicester sat on a stool at the opposite end of the table. Symbolically, he was subordinating himself to the throne that represented Elizabeth's authority in the Netherlands. Clearly, Elizabeth had made her point crystal clear to him.

83. DEMONSTRATE THANKS
Gratitude

William Cecil, the aged Lord Burghley, Elizabeth's trusted secretary of state, fell ill in 1598. As his condition worsened, Elizabeth devoted hours to his care, sitting at his bedside to feed him broth. He died on August 4, 1598.

Does a queen of England feed broth to a member of her cabinet? For Elizabeth this was an easy question to answer. Elizabeth expressed her gratitude in the most meaningful way she could think of.

84. WHY ADMIT DEFEAT?
Transform Surrender into Victory

An effective leader knows when to bow to the inevitable. A leader of genius knows how to shape that bow into a gesture of victory—a victory, moreover, in which all involved may partake.

No ruler in history was more keenly aware than Elizabeth that the phrase "absolute monarch" is a misnomer or, at least, a grossly optimistic overstatement. As a queen who ruled by divine right, she might have assumed dictatorial authority, but she understood that "divine right" was, in reality, a paper theory and that her realm was not made of paper but of people. Any exercise of power produces reactions both positive and negative.

With an eye to her kingdom's bottom line, Elizabeth always looked for ways to promote and reward loyalty without incurring costs. One means of enriching her faithful courtiers was to grant a royal monopoly, which gave the holder an exclusive right to manufacture or market a given commodity. If monopolies were powerful rewards, they were also potentially dangerous. While the holder of a monopoly was delighted—for he was now empowered to price his commodity as he chose—everyone else was resentful. The Parliament of 1598 heard many complaints about the excessive number of monopolies that had been granted. The queen, well within her rights to grant as many monopolies as she chose, could have turned a deaf ear to these complaints. Instead, she was highly responsive to them. She ordered her councillors to investigate the existing grants. As a result of their findings, Elizabeth repealed some of the monopolies— even while she granted new ones.

In October 1601, Parliament again raised the issue of excessive monopolies. This time Parliament pondered passage of an act to outlaw them. A crisis now loomed. It was, beyond doubt, a royal prerogative to grant monopolies. If an act were passed barring them, this would amount to a statutory limitation on the crown—a first big step toward the erosion of the queen's power.

Elizabeth responded to Parliament with a message that *she* would act to alleviate the evil of monopolies. Her intention was to move preemptively against legislation that would abridge her authority, yet to act without antagonizing Parliament. To maintain her power she would not challenge Parliament but, in effect, coopt it by cooperating with it. Thus, on November 28, 1601, the queen issued a proclamation repealing all monopolies judged injurious.

Elizabeth framed her proclamation with a grace that made it seem neither a preemption of a Parliamentary initiative nor a surrender to it. Indeed, the House of Commons accepted the proclamation as a great gift to the people and obtained Elizabeth's permission to send a delegation to the palace to thank her for showing them such consideration. In turn, Elizabeth made the most of this occasion. Whereas a clumsier leader might have whined that the concession made had been extorted from her, Elizabeth turned to the parliamentary delegation and begged them not to blame her if monopolies she had granted had been used to oppress any of her subjects without her knowledge.

"That my grants should be grievous to my people," she said, "and oppressions privileged under colour of our patents, our kingly dignity shall not suffer it. Yea, when I heard it, I could give no rest unto my thoughts until I had reformed it." She then rose to a height of eloquence that earned this spontaneous address to members of Parliament the popular title of "The Golden Speech."

> *I do assure you there is no prince that loves his subjects better, or whose love can countervail our love. There is no jewel, be it of never so rich a price, which I set before this jewel: I mean your love. For I do esteem it more than any treasure or riches; for that we know how to prize, but love and thanks I count invaluable. And though God hath raised me high, yet this I count the glory of my crown, that I have reigned with your loves.*

Any leader sufficiently ruthless can seize power. Through force and the threat of force, any leader can hold on to power, at least for a time. But enduring power is not taken; it is, rather, offered by those whom one leads. The skillful leader behaves in ways that induce others continually to offer this gift of power. Such behavior often requires personal restraint, a keeping of tight reins on the ego. Elizabeth was capable of such restraint, and that is one of her great virtues as a leader. She was also capable of turning this restraint, the necessity of a compromise that may even amount to a surrender, into a triumph. This was her genius.

85. A LEADER CREATES ENLIGHTENMENT
Why?

Some managers are adept at explaining the *what* and the *how* of assignments they give to subordinates, but they fail to explain the *why*. Sometimes this is the result of thoughtless omission, but often it is a product of personal policy, a feeling that it is not the place of a subordinate to ask *why*. These managers would eagerly approve the attitude of the doomed troops in Alfred, Lord Tennyson's "Charge of the Light Brigade":

> *Theirs not to make reply,*
> *Theirs not to reason why,*
> *Theirs but to do and die.*

Some managers justify this position by suggesting that discussing the *why* of an assignment invites unwanted debate on the assignment. Therefore, they just issue their orders and expect the work to be accomplished without complaint or question.

The chief problem with failing to explain the *why* is that it does not allow the person in charge to take full advantage of the intelligence, imagination, and initiative of her subordinates. Treat the people you work with like robots, and they will work like robots. Treat them as intelligent members of a team, and they will not only take an ownership pride in their work, but may well go about it more creatively. It is far easier to work and work well when a goal, a rationale, a purpose have been presented. Anything less than this is a demand for blind obedience, and an inability to see, to look ahead, and to glimpse possible alternatives never improves a result.

Elizabeth did not ask her subordinates for blind obedience. In all major enterprises, she was very clear about the *why*. When she spoke to the senior clergy of the Church of England about the necessity of their enforcing uniformity of worship, she explained the *why* with diamond clarity: "Religion is the ground on which all other matters ought to take root, and being corrupted may mar all the tree."

Enforce religious uniformity. *Why?* Because nothing is more important than the foundation of everything else. Allow fault within the foundation, and the entire structure built upon it will be fatally flawed. Armed with this explanation of the *why*, what subordinate would fail to do his utmost to carry out the assignment Elizabeth gave?

For the manager there is a challenge and a bonus attached to furnishing the *why* of each assignment. Communicating the *why* to subordinates requires knowing the *why* yourself. You may find this difficult or impossible to formulate. You may discover that there is no *why*. Or you may discover that the *why* is trivial and inadequate. In such cases, forcing yourself to formulate a *why* may convince you that the assignment needs to be revised or even discarded. It may not be worth doing. The bonus and the challenge is a rejection of mindless routine and of the bad habit of taking long-accepted procedures at face value and for granted.

86. BE A MENTOR
The Next Generation

At some time every leader has to come to terms with two related issues. The first is dealing effectively with those who hunger for the leader's power and authority—the pretenders to the throne, as it were. Elizabeth was highly effective in dealing equitably but firmly with such as these. The second issue, however, is that of succession rather than competition. A leader who builds an empire that is nothing more than a personal extension of herself leaves to posterity a poor legacy, whether it is a legacy to a nation, to a firm, or to a work group within a firm. Effective leaders provide for succession, and do so without compromising their current authority or creating dissension among prospective inheritors of the throne. It is no mean feat. Queen Elizabeth had ascended the throne of a poor and turbulent realm so torn with strife that it was hardly a nation at all. As her reign drew to a close, England enjoyed greater stability and prosperity than ever before in its history. But with neither husband nor child, the queen had left the question of succession wide open. Toward the end of her life there were at least ten possible claimants to the throne. Elizabeth and her advisers believed it critical to forestall public debate on the merits and liabilities of the contenders, lest a divisive state approaching civil war should develop. On the other hand, if Elizabeth tried to quell suspense by naming a successor, those claimants who had been excluded might well rise in rebellion, attempting to seize by arms what had been denied them. Elizabeth understood that the people dreaded the thought that she might die, leaving the succession to be bitterly and bloodily contested. But the alternatives—public debate or a nominated successor—seemed even more destructive. The queen had to find another course. Elizabeth privately sized up the likely candidates. The foreign claimants were all Catholics descended from John of Gaunt's daughters by his second wife, Constance of Castile. Among these was the daughter of Spain's Philip II, *infanta* Isabel Clara Eugenia; there was also the Portuguese duke of Braganza, and there was the eldest son of the duke of Parma. Elizabeth was not eager to bring any of these Catholic foreigners to the throne of a nation on which she had done so much to confer a stable English Protestant identity. Of the English candidates, however, none impressed the queen. As one court noble put it, "Either in their worth are they contemptible, or not liked for their sexes." (For, it seemed the country wanted "no more Queens, fearing we shall never enjoy another like this.") The two most prominent English claimants were the son of the earl of Hertford and the niece of Lord Darnley, but neither had shown much desire to succeed the queen—and, moreover, Darnley's niece, Arabella Stuart, was emotionally quite unstable.

Throughout her later reign, Elizabeth did not openly reject any of these claimants, no matter what their drawbacks. However, she kept them all in check by never allowing them sufficient power, authority, or measure of royal approval to suggest that they had been anointed to succeed her. Yet Elizabeth also avoided offending any of them or their powerful allies and supporters.

The only viable candidate in Elizabeth's eyes was James VI, king of Scotland, the son of the very woman, Mary, Queen of Scots, whose trial for treason Elizabeth reluctantly authorized and whose death warrant she had signed. Elizabeth overcame her personal feelings of distrust toward James and made an alliance with him in 1586; included with the treaty document was a sealed letter in which she promised to do nothing that would prejudice his claim to the throne unless James's actions forced her to block him. This was hardly a ringing endorsement, and James was always uneasy with this relationship. But it served Elizabeth well. It kept James and ever-rebellious Scotland on their good behavior, yet it avoided alienating the other claimants and their potentially destructive supporters and allies. For her part, Elizabeth kept up a running correspondence with James, writing to him frequently, not as one monarch to another—as an equal to an equal—but as a stern mentor to a not especially brilliant pupil. In this way, she kept James on a short leash while never quite offending him. She even managed, in the process, to teach him a few things about royal leadership.

In 1601, however, James lent diplomatic support to the short-lived rebellion of the earl of Essex, formerly the queen's favorite. Elizabeth moved swiftly to put down the rebellion, and James had every reason to believe that Elizabeth would now act to block his succession on account of his having diplomatically backed Essex. The queen, however, restrained herself. As always, she refused to act from motives of anger, disappointment, or personal vengeance. Indeed, by January 1602 she was once again corresponding with the king of Scotland and for this had clearly won his loyal gratitude. Historians have delved deeply into the court intrigue of this late period in Elizabeth's life, focusing especially on the correspondence between James and Sir Robert Cecil, who had succeeded his late father, William Cecil, as Elizabeth's secretary of state. The letters between these two were not only sent in secret, but were written in cipher. While some historians have interpreted this as an obvious conspiracy among the queen's top courtiers to ensure that James would ascend the throne whether Elizabeth approved or not, the fact is that Elizabeth herself regarded James, despite his many flaws, as the only claimant whose ascension would benefit the nation.

It is doubtful that the queen was unaware of the "conspiracy" between Cecil and James; she so thoroughly understood her responsibility as a leader to provide for her country's future that she probably allowed the conspiracy to proceed. By doing nothing to interfere she saw to it that Cecil arranged for a smooth transition. In this way, she would never be obliged personally to anoint James, thereby giving him power that would compete with hers and giving other claimants cause to muster their partisans in rebellion. Elizabeth had the strength of character to do what was right for her realm and, moreover, to do it in a brilliantly informal, unofficial manner that forestalled the civil strife that too often plagued a most disputatious island nation.

On the subject of succession, this leadership example of Elizabeth is perhaps the most difficult for others to follow. The issues raised are twofold.

First, there is the issue of succession itself. The experience of Elizabeth points up the necessity for every leader to identify and even mentor a successor and yet find a way to do it without inviting premature competition for authority and without alienating, demotivating, or wrongly motivating other hopefuls. Even more complex is the second issue: indirect leadership. Elizabeth was, above all else, a strong monarch; she aptly described herself as possessed of the outward appearance of a "weak woman" but also of the "heart and stomach of a king." One measure of Elizabeth's strength was her willingness when necessary to relinquish direct authority in a particular situation in order to achieve control through indirect means. The succession issue is a vivid example of this. Elizabeth, tacitly and indirectly, relinquished control in this matter to her secretary of state because she knew he would work to bring about the very result she desired—a result that, for important political reasons, she herself dared not directly bring about.

In the hands of anyone less experienced or less artful than Elizabeth, such a strategy of purposeful relinquishment could prove disastrous. After all, what CEO worth his salt would knowingly give away power? But Elizabeth never gave away anything. Instead, she knew how to separate the merely ego-gratifying feeling of directly exercising authority from the goals on which that authority was focused. If those goals could be reached most effectively and with the fewest unwanted side effects by forgoing the personal gratification derived from the direct exercise of power, so be it. The queen was a sufficiently great leader to allow others to exercise *their* power in order to achieve *her* ends.

O my America!
My new-found land.

—JOHN DONNE,
Elegies *(written in the 1590s)*

Six

NEW WORLDS, NEW MARKETS

GROWING THE ENTERPRISE AND CRUSHING THE COMPETITION

E*LIZABETH'S OFFICIAL ENCOURAGEMENT AND PERSONAL financial backing of such seafarers, buccaneers, explorers, and colonial entrepreneurs as John Hawkins (Hawkyns), Sir Francis Drake, Sir Humphrey Gilbert, and Sir Walter Raleigh began an economic and political expansion of England that would extend far into the nineteenth century to make it the greatest global empire in history.*

87. KNOW WHEN TO BEND— OR BREAK—THE RULES
Elizabeth, Pirate

These days, before making a major financial move, a big investment, a merger, or an acquisition, corporations must jump through multiple series of legal hoops and pass muster with any number of regulatory authorities. Recent megamergers notwithstanding, the days of the nineteenth-century "robber barons" and even of the 1980s arbitrageurs and corporate buyout cowboys seem to have come to an end. In Elizabeth's day, however, the rules of business at the highest levels were tenuous at best; indeed, they were made to be broken—for those who had the courage to break them.

In the fall of 1577, Elizabeth sent the daring British sea dog Francis Drake on what was officially described as a voyage of discovery. As an expression of affection and esteem, as well as a wish for good luck, she presented him with a cap and a green silk scarf embroidered with the words: "The Lord guide and preserve thee until the end." Drake christened one of his ships the *Elizabeth,* and the entire expedition set off without the knowledge or the approval of the queen's lord treasurer. The queen was among the investors in the enterprise.

Drake returned to England in September 1580, carrying with him the proceeds of piracy: He had captured the treasure fleet of no less than the Spanish king, Philip II.

A dispute arose among Elizabeth's councillors over the disposition of the treasure. Some, including Elizabeth's trusted secretary of state, William Cecil, Lord Burghley, insisted that it be returned immediately to Philip, that to partake in it would be to receive stolen property knowingly. Others believed the Spanish treasure was fair game for England.

As for Elizabeth, she merely suggested that Drake should come to court with whatever "souvenirs" from his expedition he thought interesting. When the Spanish ambassador insisted that Drake be punished, Elizabeth replied that she could hardly punish him without first questioning him.

Drake, in obedience to the queen's wishes, loaded his "souvenirs"—tons of treasure—on a quantity of pack horses and went to Richmond Palace, where he conversed privately with the queen for some six hours. Then when the Spanish ambassador again pressed for the return of Philip's gold, Elizabeth responded with rage, citing Spanish interference in Irish affairs (Spain was, in fact, attempting to support a rebellion) and abuse of English (Protestant) seafarers. To Drake, Elizabeth awarded £10,000 of the booty and instructed him to distribute another £10,000 among his associates. Elizabeth seized the rest of the treasure for safekeeping at the Tower of London until a decision might be reached as to its final disposition.

Later, in April 1581, Elizabeth boarded Drake's famed vessel the *Golden Hind* in company with the French envoy of the duke of Alençon, who was a prime candidate for marriage to Elizabeth. She announced to Drake that the king of Spain had asked for his head, and with these words she raised a golden sword of state, humorously making as if to execute the Spanish king's wish. She then passed the sword to the French envoy and instructed him to knight Drake Sir Francis. Thus she brought the French in on an action that would surely enrage the Spanish.

In Elizabeth's day there was no such thing as "international law," but there were commonly agreed-on rules, one of which was that seizing the property of a nation at peace was an act of high-seas piracy. True, there was no declared war between England and Spain at this time, but the Spanish were working to inflame Irish rebellion against England and were also continually harassing English traders and seafarers. Effectively, as Elizabeth saw matters, a state of war did exist, and she had no objection—in something less than an official way —to taking Spanish treasure. With an almost playful skill she defused objections to this within her own court, and she even managed to implicate the French in condoning— indeed, rewarding—the actual pirate.

Elizabeth was willing to bend and even break the rules and to accept the consequences thereof. In doing so, she not only acquired treasure and political power, but also a mystique, a reputation as a ruler whose boldness was the equal of any man's. She presented to the world an image of defiance, determination, and independence. She was willing to walk the cutlass edge of piracy, and she wanted the world to see her doing so. This had an effect of what modern military strategists would call a "force multiplier" or what modern business people would call "leveraging." England had come a long way, it was true, from a debt-burdened, dispute-torn realm, but it was still a small island nation with no standing army and very little that could be called a navy. Elizabeth behaved in a way that magnified what resources of arms and finance the nation did possess. She exhibited a *will* to act that more than over-matched that of other sovereigns.

It was a dangerous game Elizabeth played. Can the modern business leader translate the queen's boldness into a viable lesson for today? Should he even try?

It would be irresponsible to attempt to write a prescription for action based on Elizabeth's example here. Yet the leader of today must come to terms with the fact that this eminently successful leader willingly risked all on a high-handed, highly provocative, and ethically questionable (perhaps illegal) venture. At the very least, the lesson to be drawn from this may be an awareness of the role unconventional action plays in high-stakes leadership. Piracy, for Elizabeth, militarily unable to risk a formal declaration of war against Spain—and, indeed, unwilling to challenge another monarch so openly—was a way of thinking outside the box. Whatever else it was, we should regard it as a highly creative response to an extremely difficult situation.

88. PROMOTE WITHOUT PREJUDICE
"The Service of All Sorts"

Elizabeth took great pains to ensure that she marshaled the services and loyalty of the great nobility of her realm, but she never allowed a hereditary title to take precedence over sheer ability. To a diplomat visiting from the Netherlands the queen remarked with pride on her ability to "divine the humour of everyone" and that she believed it wise "for her to make use of the service of all sorts, great and small," for "she knew how to elevate lesser men when they deserved it." For Elizabeth, her perception of performance and ability ultimately determined whether a man would be promoted in her service. In this way, commoners and minor nobles sometimes found themselves elevated to positions of great importance on the strength of their actual achievements. The support she gave Francis Drake, for example, a poor farm lad and seafarer, is a case in point. For England, his singlehanded exploits against colonial Spain really were worth those of an army.

89. NO LEADER IS A SOLO ACT
Human Resources

In a portrait painted after the defeat of the Spanish Armada, Elizabeth is depicted with her hand resting on a globe, her finger pointing to the Americas, up to this time the exclusive province of the Spanish. In background insets to the portrait are depicted the English fleet in full and glorious sail and the Spanish Armada, storm-tossed and wrecked.

The portrait is instructive. Its message is this: Under Elizabeth's leadership, England had defeated Spain and was on its way to conquering the New World. Contemplate further the inset of the British fleet, and the import of the message is further refined: *Elizabeth* did not defeat the Spanish and would not conquer a New World. She commanded the *fleet* to victory and would continue to command it to conquest.

By definition no leader is a solo act. What she achieves is also and in large part the achievement of others. For Elizabeth, one of the most remarkable of those "others" was a man named Francis Drake.

He was born sometime between 1540 and 1543 on the estate of Lord Francis Russell of Devonshire. His father was one of Russell's tenant farmers. During a Catholic uprising of 1549, the Protestant Drake family had to flee the west country, and they settled in Kent in the southeast. Homeless, the family took refuge in the hulk of an abandoned navy ship moored in an estuary of the Thames. At age thirteen Drake apprenticed to the master of a small vessel sailing the coastal waters from one North Sea port to another. It was a hard and useful apprenticeship, for the North Sea was stormy and the coastline hazardous. Drake learned the skills of pilotage under the most demanding conditions. When the captain of his vessel died, he left the ship to Drake.

Drake was distantly related to the wealthy and powerful Hawkins (Hawkyns) family of Plymouth, Devon, who had just begun investing in New World trade. Eager for adventure and wealth, and eager also to penetrate the New World claimed by Catholic Spain, Drake, aged about twenty-three, sold his coastal vessel to enlist in the service of the Hawkinses. His early experiences in the West Indies increased his hatred and resentment of the Spanish, who routinely abused foreign traders by impounding their cargoes and sometimes detained captains and crews. At San Juan de Ulúa, off the coast of Mexico, he and his crew were ambushed by the Spanish. Drake escaped unharmed, but many of his crew were killed. From this point on Drake became a "privateer," in effect a practitioner of state-sanctioned piracy, who boldly preyed on Spanish shipping.

Privateering was an accepted practice among the nations of renaissance Europe, although it tempted a declaration of war against the sponsoring country and certainly presented great peril to the privateer, who, if captured, would be punished as a pirate. In 1572, Elizabeth presented Drake with an official privateering commission, and she also personally invested in his piratical voyages. Drake set off for America in two small vessels, *Pasha* and *Swan*, and plundered the important Spanish town of Nombre de Dios, Panama, making away with enough treasure to enrich himself as well as his investors.

He returned to England rich and famous—although Queen Elizabeth could not fully and officially acknowledge his achievement since she had, for the time being, reached an accord with Philip II of Spain. The queen made clear to Drake the current circumstances, and he wisely decided to bide his time before reembarking on privateering against Spain. Instead, he served Elizabeth by providing naval support for the earl of Essex who was fighting rebels in Ireland. But in 1577, Elizabeth called on him again for the talents he had already amply demonstrated. He was named to lead an expedition around the world. The objective of the mission was to pass around South America and through the Strait of

Magellan to explore the coast beyond. He was to conclude treaties with any peoples who lay south of the Spanish sphere of control, and he was to look for an unknown continent believed to be in the unexplored reaches of the South Pacific.

At this point the temporary rapprochement with Philip II had dissolved, and Elizabeth frankly commissioned Drake to do as much damage to the Spanish as he could. She told him that she "would gladly be revenged on the King of Spain for divers injuries that I have received." As usual, Elizabeth also backed Drake with part of her personal fortune.

He kept the expedition small, five ships manned by no more than two hundred men total. His flagship, christened the *Pelican* and renamed by Drake the *Golden Hind*, was small at merely one hundred tons. By the spring of 1578 his modest flotilla had reached the coast of Brazil. There Drake discovered a mutinous plot against him, which he dealt with summarily by trying and executing its leader, one Thomas Doughty. Assuring himself of the loyalty of those who remained, he abandoned two of his ships (which had served mainly to carry stores), and on August 21, 1578, now with three vessels, he entered the Straits of Magellan. No sooner did he reach the Pacific than a fierce storm separated the *Golden Hind* from the other craft. Ultimately, it was only Drake's flagship that sailed into the Pacific and up the coast of South America.

It proved sufficient to do the job. The Spaniards, confident that no hostile power would ever threaten their Pacific possessions, left them entirely undefended. Drake plundered towns and vessels—gathering a haul of gold and silver bullion, Spanish coins, jewels, and pearls—in South America and then sailed northward, all the way to present-day Vancouver, British Columbia, in search of a Northwest Passage back to the Atlantic. Failing to find this, he sailed south to an anchorage just north of modern San Francisco. He claimed California for Elizabeth, christening it New Albion.

In July 1579, Drake sailed west across the Pacific, touching the Philippines and the Moluccas, where he concluded a treaty that gave the English exclusive rights to the trade in spices—at the time a commodity even more valuable than gold. He sailed on to Java, then across the Indian Ocean and the Cape of Good Hope. On September 26, 1580, Drake returned to Plymouth Harbor. Half of the crew of the *Golden Hind* had perished, but Drake and the survivors were incomparably rich. Drake had also earned the distinction of being the first captain to sail around the world. (Ferdinand Magellan's crew had completed a circumnavigation earlier, but Magellan himself had been killed.)

Elizabeth bestowed a knighthood upon Drake, doing so on the deck of *Golden Hind* itself, and gave him her sustained support. Drake became mayor of Plymouth in 1581 and enjoyed great popularity as a hero of England, but he also incurred the envy and enmity of many important people. He was, after all, a farmer's son who lacked the polished grace of a London courtier and who spoke with the heavy rustic accent of a west country man. Elizabeth did not share the class prejudices of her courtiers. In 1585, in defiance of the advice of such high-born seafarers as Sir Richard Grenville and Sir Martin Frobisher, she demonstrated her continued confidence and support by naming Drake commander of a fleet of twenty-five ships that would attack the overseas empire of Spain.

As usual, Elizabeth's confidence and judgment proved well founded. Drake captured Santiago in the Cape Verde Islands, Cartagena in Colombia, St. Augustine in Florida, and Santo Domingo in Hispaniola. The effect of these triumphs was devastating to Spain. The nation's credit all but collapsed as the Bank of Spain went broke; the Bank of Venice (which had made immense loans to Philip II) nearly went broke; and the important Bank of Augsburg refused to extend any more credit to Philip. Elizabeth's own secretary of state, Lord Burghley, had advised her against sending Drake on a mission he was sure would fail. Elizabeth knew her man better than Burghley did, and now the secretary admitted to his queen that "Sir Francis Drake is a fearful man to the King of Spain."

Of course, Philip did not take these attacks lying down. In 1586, he began to speak of what he called the "Enterprise of England," a massive invasion aimed at returning England to the Catholic sphere of Rome. In 1587, however, Elizabeth commissioned Drake to "impeach the provisions of Spain," and she fitted him out with thirty ships, with which Drake attacked the Spanish harbor of Cadiz. In a mere thirty-six hours, Drake destroyed thousands upon thousands of tons of shipping as well as supplies—the core of a great "armada" that Philip had planned to hurl against England.

In commissioning Drake on his anti-Spanish expeditions, Elizabeth deliberately framed the missions in the vivid personal terms of righteous vengeance, and she further motivated Drake with promises of material reward, recognition, and full royal support. Yet the strategy that underlay this was not so much vengeful or personal as it was brilliantly logical. Elizabeth attacked Spain economically. Privateering "impeach[ed] the provisions of Spain"; it cut off its supplies of goods, of ships, of armament, and, most damaging of all, its supply of credit. Traditionally, monarchs fought their wars and made their conquests with large and costly armies. Elizabeth, in contrast, discovered the principle of leverage. She used Drake and his handful of ships in lieu of a vast army to attack not the people of Spain but the treasure of Spain— the very fuel on which conquest depends.

Yet, while Drake had severely crippled Spain's war-making power, he had not killed it. By July 1588, much delayed by Drake's action, the Spanish Armada was in the English Channel. Drake had been appointed vice admiral under Lord Howard to defend against the invasion. Elizabeth had chosen Howard rather than Drake because she knew that he enjoyed the full confidence and respect of *all* the English nobility. She also knew that Howard had full confidence in Drake and would give him the widest possible scope for action. As vice admiral, Drake was free to operate with his accustomed dash and brilliance. Drake not only captured a rich prize during a great sea fight in the English Channel, but he used fire ships—unmanned hulks deliberately set ablaze—to force the ships of the Armada out of Calais where they had taken refuge. Thus exposed, they could more readily be attacked. Even more devastating, however, is that the Armada was also exposed to the elements, and a fierce Channel storm completed the destruction of the Spanish fleet.

Would Sir Francis Drake have achieved greatness under a sovereign other than Elizabeth I? Perhaps. Yet it is to Drake that historians have always pointed as the embodiment of the "Elizabethan" ideals of bold expansion. Always that adjective, *Elizabethan*, is attached to his name and his exploits. For it was the leadership of Elizabeth that empowered his achievement at its inception as well as on a continuing basis. She supported, defended, enabled, and encouraged him. If Drake extended the queen's rule into a New World and at the expense of her realm's chief rival, it was the stamp of this queen's spirit that helped him accomplish it. A leader is an enabler.

"*I am your anointed Queen.*
I will never be by violence
constrained to do anything."

—ELIZABETH,
in a speech to Parliament, 1566

Seven

"THE HEART AND STOMACH OF A KING"

TURNING CRISIS INTO TRIUMPH

E*LIZABETH WAS NOT A WARLIKE LEADER; SHE GREATLY preferred the force of adept diplomacy to the force of arms. Threatened with invasion or other violent crisis, however, she rose to heights of eloquence, courage, and inspiration that would not be equaled in England until the World War II leadership of Winston Churchill. Elizabeth transformed threat into national strength, and crisis into collective opportunity.*

90. DUCK AND COVER? NO WAY
Early Triumph

In 1560, twenty-six-year-old Elizabeth, in year two of her reign, scored a profound triumph in Scotland. Ruled by Mary, Queen of Scots and her French husband, Scotland was a threat to England and was prime territory for use by hostile powers as a staging area preparatory to an invasion of England. When the French did indeed lodge troops in Scotland and Spain threatened to do the same, Elizabeth had a difficult decision to make. She could sit idly by and hope for the best, or she could intervene in Scotland, using her army and navy to defy France and Spain, thereby risking war with the two greatest powers in Europe.

Inaction, hunkering down, taking cover often seems the safest possible course. This, however, is an illusion. To duck and cover typically transforms one into a target—and not even a *moving* target. After much agonizing, therefore, Elizabeth chose to intervene.

By the Treaty of Upsetlington, Elizabeth had pledged to give no aid to Protestant rebels in Scotland. Now she secretly sent money to the rebels, and she authorized her admiral, Sir William Winter, to blockade the Firth of Forth. Winter captured ships that had been sent to supply munitions to the French army in Scotland. Then, in March 1560, the queen authorized an English army to invade Scotland. Although the major battle at Leith ended in the defeat of this force, it did motivate the negotiation of the Treaty of Edinburgh by Elizabeth's trusted and brilliant secretary of state, William Cecil, the First Baron Burghley. By this treaty the French agreed to withdraw from Scotland and let the Scots settle their own religion. In return, the English withdrew their demand for the immediate return of Calais, which had been lost to the French during the reign of Mary I. Burghley also agreed to forgo, at least for the present, any demand for compensation from Mary, Queen of Scots, who had dared to include the English heraldic arms in her own coat of arms. Burghley also agreed to dissolve the alliance between Elizabeth and the Scots Protestant leaders known as the Lords of the Congregation.

As authorized by Elizabeth, these concessions made it possible for the French to save face by claiming a compromise settlement in the Treaty of Edinburgh. Actually, the treaty represented an English triumph: The French presence had been removed from Scotland. With this, the impending Spanish threat was also removed. Moreover, the treaty put in place the mechanism that enabled the Scottish Parliament to legislate a Protestant state religion for Scotland despite the Catholicism and Catholic political allegiances of Mary, Queen of Scots.

The Scottish victory demonstrated Elizabeth's courage as a leader and her preference for action (albeit always careful and considered action) over inaction. She refused to allow herself or her nation to drift at the mercy of events but instead risked a proactive response by taking preemptive action. The stakes were high, for she might have brought down upon England the military might of France as well as Spain. But she knew that Spain was preoccupied with rebellion in the Netherlands (at the time a Spanish province), and she gambled that France would not fight her alone, at least not over Scotland.

We often forget that leadership sometimes requires genuine courage, a willingness to weigh risk against reward and, even in a close call, sometimes to opt for risk. Beyond the fact of Elizabeth's courage is the care she took to evaluate the situation before acting. She also ensured that she was well advised by William Cecil, who she knew could be trusted to make the most of the resources she was placing at risk. Elizabeth was not deceived by the illusion of prudence and safety presented by the prospect of inaction; however, she also chose to avoid acting impulsively or blindly. The choice to intervene bought her nation a powerful negotiating chip.

91. ACTION SPEAKS LOUDER...
Attraction to Action

History has bestowed on Thomas Seymour, lord high admiral of England from 1547 to 1549, a bad reputation. Seymour began his climb up the Tudor court ladder as a result of his sister Jane's marriage to King Henry VIII in 1536, receiving fairly minor employment at court and on certain second-rank diplomatic missions. In 1544, he was named commander of the fleet stationed in the English Channel for operations against France; he later became a baron, lord high admiral, and a member of the king's Privy Council. In 1547, Seymour moved his career even further by marrying the sixth wife of Henry VIII—and now Henry's widow—Catherine Parr. The dashing Seymour gained great influence over the young and sickly King Edward VI and shamelessly used his office to make highly profitable—and wholly illegal—deals with the

Channel pirates. When Catherine Parr died in September 1548, Seymour resolved to make the ultimate career move: marriage to Princess Elizabeth. A scandal arose over an alleged sexual relationship between Seymour and the adolescent Elizabeth, but these rumors—almost certainly unfounded— were far less troubling to Edward Seymour, Protector of the underage King Edward VI, than the prospect of his unprincipled brother becoming, through marriage, an heir to the throne. At last, Edward Seymour persuaded Edward VI that Thomas should be arrested on thirty-three charges of treason, which included scheming to abduct the young king, having married Catherine Parr in such haste that any child she bore could have been Henry's, and, finally, scheming to marry Elizabeth. In short order, Thomas Seymour was found guilty and beheaded in 1549. Elizabeth was cast under a cloud of suspicion and subjected to relentless inquisition. As for Edward Seymour, having sought security by disposing of his brother, he had inadvertently sown the seeds of his own destruction. His extreme severity toward his brother was used by rival politicians as evidence against *him*. These rivals engineered his removal from office later in the year.

While it is doubtful that Thomas Seymour had actually done anything to warrant losing his head, it is beyond doubt that he was a rogue and a dangerous man. It is also beyond doubt that Elizabeth was attracted to him, not so much romantically—though there almost certainly was a flirtation—but imaginatively. To her he represented a key aspect of leadership: boldness of action, an ability and willingness to get things done, to make her own rules, to slash through political complexities and bureaucratic red tape. Of course, as a mature woman, as a queen, Elizabeth would realize that such qualities, while essential to leadership, were not alone sufficient for leadership. Judgment, restraint, and, ultimately, a certain selflessness were also necessary. Yet all her life Elizabeth would be attracted to this most dynamic core ingredient of leadership—action— which she recognized, celebrated, rewarded, and sometimes even punished—in such men as Sir Walter Raleigh, Sir Francis Drake, Sir John Hawkins, and the second earl of Essex.

92. BEWARE WASTEFUL CONFLICT
The Sieve of War

Of war Elizabeth once remarked: "It is a sieve, that spends as it receives to little purpose."

In war, Elizabeth was a bold and courageous sovereign, a leader who inspired her troops. However, she did everything possible to avoid war, not out of any pacifist sentiment or scruples but because, in all things, she abhorred waste. And she reckoned war inherently wasteful.

Most creative leaders look for ways to avoid costly conflict. This does not mean buckling to pressure from the outside or hoisting the white flag at the first sign of trouble. But it does mean looking for ways to transform us-versus-them situations into cooperative and collaborative we-together scenarios. It calls for thinking beyond confrontations as zero-sum games, and instead creating encounters that can result in a win for both sides. Often, it calls for reining in one's ego and controlling one's temper. Always, it calls for focusing on objectives and goals rather than on personalities.

Elizabeth's secretary of state, William Cecil, Lord Burghley, put it this way: "Seek peace but prepare for war."

93. THE SOLDIER IS THE ARMY
"The Poor Soldiers"

The lot of the common foot soldier has never been an easy one. In the sixteenth century, it was particularly hard. When Elizabeth discovered that the troops she had sent to the Netherlands to fight in the Protestant struggle against Spain were not being paid, she wrote to their commander, Robert Dudley, the earl of Leicester:

It frets me not a little that the poor soldiers that hourly venture life should want [lack] their due, that well deserve rather reward. And look in whom the fault may duly be proved, let them smart therefore. And if the Treasurer be found untrue or negligent according to desert he shall be used; though you know my old wont, that love not to discharge from office without desert, God forbid. I pray you let this bearer know what may be learned herein; and for this treasure I have joined [enjoined—that is, commanded] Sir Thomas Shirley to see all this money discharged in due sort where it needeth and behoveth.

Elizabeth understood well what General George S. Patton would observe some four centuries after her about the source of the effectiveness of a military organization: "The soldier is the army," he said. Learning that her troops were not being paid, she took immediate action:

1. She informed their senior field commander, Leicester.
2. She made it clear to Leicester that the matter was of top-priority concern to her.
3. She directed Leicester to determine who was responsible for the failure to pay the soldiers.
4. She informed Leicester that those responsible would suffer reprimand: "smart therefore."
5. She informed Leicester that she was prepared to "discharge from office" the army's treasurer if he was found remiss.
6. She dispatched a man (Sir Thomas Shirley) personally to attend to the proper disbursement of the funds.

Here is the essence of leadership:

- High regard for subordinates
- An understanding of basic motivation as well as basic justice
- A willingness to take responsibility
- A willingness to demand responsibility from others
- A willingness to correct a faulty situation
- A willingness to take positive, quick, and aggressive action

94. GET IN THE TRENCHES
Frontline

On July 19, 1588, the ships—some 130 vessels—of the great Spanish Armada were sighted in the English Channel. As England braced for invasion, Elizabeth refused to hole up in the guarded safety of London and instead went to Tilbury, where the bulk of the army was camped, girding to defend the island kingdom. As Elizabeth walked through the encampment, the army fell on its knees. It was said, too, that Elizabeth wept to behold them. She took a meal with her general under the canvas of a tent, and the next day she donned the breastplate of a cavalry officer and (according to an eyewitness) rode "on prancing steed attired like an angel bright."

A leader is present at the front lines. A leader ensures that he is seen. A leader particularly ensures that he is seen taking the same risks as those he leads.

95. HOPE FOR THE BEST BUT PREPARE FOR SOMETHING LESS
Practical Faith

When, in 1593, Parliament was predicting the onslaught of a new Spanish Armada, Elizabeth addressed the members with words of encouragement and faith:

You have heard in the beginning of this Parliament,
some doubt [worry] of danger, more than I would have
you to fear. For mine own part I protest I never feared
and what fear was my heart never knew. For I knew
that my cause was ever just and it standeth upon a
sure foundation—that I should not fail, God assisting
the quarrel of the righteous, and such as are but
to defend.

Elizabeth inspired and assured Parliament with a speech that in some ways anticipated Franklin Delano Roosevelt's first inaugural address when he told his countrymen that "the only thing we have to fear is fear itself." She also spoke persuasively of something many leaders, before and since, have spoken of: faith in the righteousness of their cause. It is important for a leader to define and inspire faith and confidence in the efficacy of faith, yet it is folly to rely passively on faith alone. When Czar Nicholas II of Russia, confronted with revolution, was asked what to do, his reply was simply this: "God will provide." He did little or nothing, his government toppled, and he and his family were ultimately massacred.

Even buoyed by her deep and abiding faith, Elizabeth was never passive. Having told Parliament that God would protect England, she immediately toured the coastal towns and meticulously inspected the ships that would defend England. She spoke in particular to the lords-lieutenant of the coastal counties: "You that in the shires have the leading of the most choice and serviceable men under your bands, let me charge you that you see them sufficiently exercised and trained, and that all decays of armour be presently repaired and made sufficient."

Have faith, was Elizabeth's message, but train your men and be certain that the armor they wear is in good repair. The successful leader is a believer, but always a *practical* believer who never relies on any one faith or force or influence to carry the day. Faith and practical preparation go hand in hand.

As it turned out, this new Spanish Armada never got out of port. Storms prevented its sailing.

96. STEP IN AND HELP
Intervention

Bad weather proved an ally in the British fight against the Spanish, once helping to destroy the ships of the armada in the English Channel and once keeping a new armada from deploying at all. However, this same bad weather, during the 1590s, ruined English harvests and created a severe food shortage as well as a period of inflation. Elizabeth took action.

Although she believed that the growth of England depended on the motivation of a capitalist market-driven economy, she ordered local sheriffs and justices of the peace to enforce the sale of grain at certain reasonable prices. The wealthy were asked to go supperless on Wednesdays and Fridays, donating their meal or the price of their meal to the poor. Elizabeth also lifted import duties on wheat and rye. These had been put in place to encourage the development of English agriculture. Now, however, the most important thing was to ensure a sufficient supply of bread. Merchants were encouraged to buy foreign grain in the port towns.

It must have galled Elizabeth to intervene in the marketplace, which she rightly believed was the engine driving the growth and greatness of England. Yet she did not hesitate to do just this when dire circumstances called for emergency action. A large part of Elizabeth's effectiveness as a leader was the manner in which she combined the idealism of a visionary with the sound judgment of a practical manager. She also possessed the will to stay the course as well as the good sense to know when a detour was necessary. In this she calls to mind a leader like Franklin D. Roosevelt as compared to his predecessor, Herbert Hoover. Faced with the Great Depression, Hoover, who had built his reputation as a humanitarian relief administrator after World War I, was certainly not unsympathetic. However, he lacked the imagination to see that a compromise of certain capitalist and democratic ideals was called for precisely to save capitalism and democracy. His successor, Roosevelt, suffered from no such shortage of imagination. Like Elizabeth, he boldly put sweeping emergency measures into action. A leader must never be unprincipled but must never allow himself to be straitjacketed by principle.

97. NO NEED TO SHOUT
Articulate Anger

In the summer of 1597, an ambassador from the king of Poland called at the royal court in Greenwich. Elizabeth received him graciously, and the young man began his speech in the international language, Latin. The address to the queen was not the customary complimentary speech of the representative of one sovereign to another sovereign but instead was a diatribe on how England's war with Spain was negatively affecting the merchants and trade of Poland, violating, the ambassador said, the "law of nature and of nations."

Elizabeth had been, in effect, blindsided. Expecting a pleasant compliment, she had received instead an impertinent slap in the face. Livid, she began her reply to the young ambassador.

Most people find it difficult to express anger articulately. Rage and eloquence rarely go together. If they did, few fistfights (or worse) would ever break out. At best, when angered, most of us manage enough self-control to sputter a few expletives. Not so Elizabeth. In what witnesses described as flawless Latin, she delivered to the ambassador a reasoned dressing down:

> *How I have been deceived! I was expecting a diplomatic mission, but you have brought me a quarrel! By virtue of your testimonials [credentials] I have received you as an ambassador, but I have you instead a challenger. Never in*

my life have I heard such audacity. I marvel, indeed I marvel at so great and unprecedented impertinence in public. Nor can I believe that had your King been here he would have spoken in such words.

This expression of displeasure was withering enough, but Elizabeth continued, twisting the knife by degrees:

But if he had, indeed, happened, which I can scarcely credit, to entrust some such matter to your hands, even though the King is young and a King not by birth but by election— and newly elected at that—he would show himself as having a very imperfect understanding of the manner in which such matters are handled between Princes, a manner observed towards us by his betters and which he will perhaps observe in future. As for yourself, you give me the impression of having studied many books, but not yet of having graduated to the books of Princes, rather remaining ignorant of the dealings between Kings.

Your king is too young and inexperienced, Elizabeth suggested, to know how to deal with other monarchs. Moreover, he was elected, not born to his office, so perhaps cannot be expected to know how to act like a *true* king. Maybe he will now learn his lesson. As for you, his ambassador, you may have read widely, but you have learned little.

A leader insists on being treated like a leader. She does not tolerate disrespect for her office. Yet in responding to such disrespect, she is careful to avoid lowering herself to the level of her adversary. Elizabeth's reply is both withering and eminently civilized. Moreover, it is all delivered in the courtly international language, Latin.

Having addressed the breach of decorum and respect, Elizabeth launched into the actual substance of the ambassador's complaint:

> *As to the law of nature and of nations of which you make so much mention, know that the law of nature and of nations is thus: when war is declared between Kings, either may cut the other's lines of supply, no matter where they run from, and neither may they make it a precondition of their losses that these be made good. This, I say, is the law of nature and of nations.*

With crystal clarity Elizabeth defined the "law of nature and nations," turning this phrase against the very person who hurled it at her in the first place. What is the law of nature and nations? In war, supply lines are fair targets and may be cut without regard to the effect this may have on third parties.

Anger is natural in many situations, and there is little use in trying to avoid or evade what is natural. However, while a leader does not deny strong emotion, neither does he allow himself to be mastered by it. True eloquence is founded on the ability to channel powerful emotion into articulate expression. It is a leadership skill worth studying, developing, and honing.

"*I will make you shorter by the head.*"

—ELIZABETH,
quoted in Frederick Chamberlin,
The Sayings of Queen Elizabeth, *1923*

Eight

REBELLION

HOLDING ONTO THE POWER

Elizabeth *always preferred leadership by consensus and accommodation, but she did not hesitate to draw a clear and absolute line beyond which she would not yield and across which none could encroach. Those who did were dealt with swiftly and decisively.*

98. DEMAND MORE THAN WORDS
"We Only Require Performance"

Elizabeth had only to look at a map to understand much about her nation's political position in the world. The England whose throne Elizabeth ascended had no standing army and virtually no navy. It was protected from invasion principally by a geographical fact: its status as an island.

However, Elizabeth did not rule an entire island, but half of one, for Scotland to the north was a wild place, with its own monarch—though it was a land widely considered ungovernable.

Elizabeth had little desire to take over and attempt to govern Scotland, but she knew that she could not ignore this realm, either. For if Scotland made an alliance with some other power, say Spain or France, England would lose the protection afforded by its island status. A foreign power allied with Scotland could use this northern region as a vast staging area from which to launch and maintain an invasion. In the sixteenth century, an amphibious invasion was monumentally difficult to execute, but land-borne invasions were practically matters of routine.

Mary Stuart—Mary, Queen of Scots—was the only child of King James V of Scotland and his French wife, Mary of Guise. The death of the king just six days after Mary's birth elevated her to the Scottish throne. Her great-uncle, Elizabeth's father, Henry VIII, tried to secure control of her, but Mary's mother was named regent instead, and she sent the girl to France for her education. Thus Mary grew up as a Frenchwoman rather than a Scot, and this was profoundly troubling to Elizabeth, who feared that her kinswoman, who had married Francis, the son of the French king and queen, would conclude an alliance with France that could lead to an invasion.

And there was more. Although a Stuart, Mary also had Tudor blood in her veins, which put her next in line to the

English throne after Elizabeth. Indeed, those English Catholics who looked on Elizabeth as a bastard regarded Mary as already the legitimate queen of England. And she was, quite literally, an attractive choice. Although Elizabeth was a pretty young woman, Mary was an extraordinary figure: extremely tall (at five-eleven in an age when very few *men* reached this height), slender, her hair reddish gold (not unlike Elizabeth's), her eyes a haunting amber. To many she seemed the ideal of courtly beauty, and her physical presence made her that much more compelling as a prospective queen of England.

Elizabeth was anxious that Mary should ratify the Treaty of Edinburgh, concluded in 1560 and specifying the removal of all French forces from Scotland. Stubbornly, Mary delayed ratifying the treaty, though she offered all manner of professions of amity and loyalty to Elizabeth. In exasperation, Elizabeth wrote to her on August 16, 1560: "We assure you your answer is no satisfaction, we only require performance of your promise . . ." Elizabeth could not afford to content herself with words; she wanted deeds: the ratification. Again, in September, she called for ratification, and yet again in November: "We only require the ratification of the treaty passed by your hand. When princesses treat openly by assembly of ambassadors [instead of person to person], the world, especially the subjects of both, judge the amity not sound, but shaken or crazed."

There comes a time when a leader must force the issue by calling for an absolute commitment. Elizabeth believed that there would be no final and enduring settlement of the question of French forces in Scotland until Mary personally ratified the Treaty of Edinburgh, cementing the amity between Scotland and England, not through an "assembly of ambassadors" but by firm agreement between two sovereigns.

Although the Treaty of Edinburgh did go into effect, Mary never ratified it herself, and this was the origin of the deepest rift between the two sovereigns. Elizabeth refused to trust words when deeds were called for.

99. AVOID IMPULSE
"And Stay Our Judgement"

After the Protestant Scots lords deposed Mary, Queen of Scots, following the violent death of her husband, Darnley, the beautiful queen was held captive for nearly a year. On May 2, 1568, she managed to escape and to rally an army in her defense. These troops, however, were defeated at the Battle of Langside, whereupon Mary and a few followers made a dash for England. There she sought asylum from Elizabeth.

Elizabeth was now in an awkward and dangerous position. To begin with, Mary wanted Elizabeth to help restore her to the Scottish throne. Elizabeth knew that if she did not help, Mary would most likely seek aid from the French—and that would undo what had been accomplished by the Treaty of Edinburgh, for French troops would again be in Scotland, presenting the threat of invasion of England. Yet if Elizabeth did offer aid, then the Scots lords might call on the French. Either way, there was for England risk without tangible reward.

Another possibility was to bring Mary to Elizabeth's court and there offer her protection and political, if not military, support for her restoration. This, however, presented two problems. First, the charismatic Scottish queen would become a focus for English Catholics, who might become emboldened to rebel. Second, it would not be seemly for Elizabeth and her court if she harbored a woman publicly accused of having murdered her husband.

Elizabeth faced a complex crisis. Mary was a dangerous rival. The Scots lords had deposed her and her religion, which, on the face of it, were both positive occurrences for England. To protect or restore Mary would, in many ways, be detrimental to England. Yet Elizabeth felt that she could not let stand, let alone in any way validate, an unlawful revolution against a kinswoman and, more important, a fellow monarch.

Elizabeth resorted to the common law of her country. She ordered Mary "lodged"—in effect, held prisoner—in the north of England, at York, far from the London court. In October 1568, an inquiry was convened at York to determine Mary's guilt or innocence of complicity in Darnley's murder and to look into the activities of the earl of Moray, regent to the infant James and therefore the person who presently ran the government of Scotland. When these proceedings proved inconclusive, Elizabeth ordered the inquiry transferred to Westminster, and on December 7, Moray produced what a lawyer of today would call "the smoking gun." It was a small gilded box—or "casket"—decorated with the letter *F*, initial of Francis II, Mary's first husband. Inside were letters supposedly written by Mary to the Fourth Earl of Bothwell, the man with whom she was accused of having plotted Darnley's murder. The letters showed that Mary and Bothwell had been lovers before the Darnley murder. The Scottish queen protested that the letters were forgeries (and historians have been arguing about this claim for more than four centuries), but Elizabeth was now acutely distressed. Many of her advisers could see no reason for such distress, however. The "casket letters," they said, were ample evidence to do away with Mary forever—and without suffering repercussions from English Catholics, Scots Catholics, or the French. Her execution would now be a criminal matter and not a political one. Not even Mary's ardent religious or political advocates would be able to rally supporters to the cause of a martyred adulteress and murderer.

For Elizabeth, the immediate trial and execution of Mary for murder would have been a quick fix to a long-vexing problem. But Elizabeth instinctively shunned quick fixes. She looked instead for solutions that would be both enduring and just. Whatever her ethical and moral basis for seeking justice, she also understood as a leader that quick fixes, if tainted and unfair, poisoned a people and eroded authority over time. It would have been easy to give in to temptation. She had advisers telling her to do just that. Instead, Elizabeth wrote to Mary:

We have been very sorry of long time for your mishaps and great troubles, so find we our sorrows now double in beholding such things as are produced to prove yourself cause of all the same; and our grief herein is also increased in what we did not think at any time to have seen or heard such matters of so great appearance and moment to charge and condemn you. Nevertheless both in friendship, nature and justice we are moved to cover these matters and stay our judgement, and not gather any sense thereof to your prejudice before we may hear of your direct answer thereunto.

It looks bad for you, Elizabeth was saying, but, rest assured, no matter how bad it looks, I will not judge you until I have heard your side.

Once a leader puts expedience above fairness, his authority crumbles away like something rotten. Crises have to be dealt with in a timely manner, and opportunities, too, must be seized. But false steps in the present tend to compound into disaster at some future time. An effective leader does not fail to deal with the present, but in so doing he takes care not to lose the future.

100. A LEADER SETS THE LIMITS
The Limit of Conciliation

Late in 1568, news reached Elizabeth of a rebellion brewing in the north of England. Its object was to overthrow Elizabeth and replace her with Mary, Queen of Scots. Many of Elizabeth's advisers counseled a conciliatory course, a course of leniency and mercy. Elizabeth, always a moderate, listened attentively to the advice, but she determined that the rebels had crossed a line beyond conciliation. Having decided this, she proposed to act with military force to put down the rebellion quickly and decisively.

Each leader must define limits of acceptable behavior and acceptable performance. Readily redefining these limits in the interest of "conciliation" is a risky strategy that threatens to undermine authority and the standards of leadership.

101. DO NOT ACT PREMATURELY, ACT DECISIVELY
Treachery

It was discovered that Mary, Queen of Scots, still being held in custody in the north of England, her life preserved by the good graces of Elizabeth, had been writing regularly to the French and Spanish ambassadors during 1583–84. The communication was totally clandestine, conducted in cipher or with invisible ink; the messages themselves were carried in hollowed-out shoe heels or the linings of clothing. In November 1583, a prominent Catholic nobleman named Francis Throckmorton was arrested. His papers were searched, and among them was found a pair of lists, one containing the names of nobles who could be counted on to rise against Elizabeth in behalf of Mary and the other listing English ports at which troops could be landed for an invasion of England. When Don Bernardino de Mendoza, Spain's ambassador, was implicated in the papers, Elizabeth ordered him to leave the country despite his protests that King Philip II would have his revenge against Elizabeth and her realm. By January 1584 it had become clear that numerous plots were being hatched against the life of Elizabeth, and Parliament assembled a Bond of Association to protect the queen. The bond consisted of thousands of gentlemen from all over England who swore that they would exact immediate vengeance against anyone who harmed Elizabeth.

Characteristically, Elizabeth downplayed the threat to herself. She delayed passage of a bill to enforce the Bond of Association and also delayed a bill to introduce harsher penalties against Jesuits and seminary priests. She did not want to compromise her negotiating strength as she discussed ways of restoring Mary to the Scottish throne in joint rule with her son, James VI. Even now Elizabeth was more interested in preserving the rights of a fellow anointed sovereign than in punishing Mary.

But just as James VI definitively rejected the notion of sharing the throne with his mother, the assassination plans of

Dr. William Parry, a member of Parliament, were discovered. Parry had discussed with an associate the possibility of killing the queen as she walked in St. James's Park.

Parry was arrested and convicted of treason. Under English law, traitors, including would-be regicides, were to be executed by hanging, after which the body was to be drawn and quartered—spread-eagled and butchered. Often, the executioner saw to it that the hanging would not be immediately lethal so that the condemned man suffered dismemberment while still alive and at least semiconscious. Even this gruesome punishment, however, was not sufficient for Parliament, which beseeched Elizabeth to deal with Parry in no ordinary way but to allow them to invent some novel, more horrible form of torture and slow death. Moreover, Parliament would make it all perfectly legal by enacting a special law.

Elizabeth replied that Parry was to be dealt with according to existing English law—no more, no less.

The queen was not so foolish as to pardon Parry or commute his sentence. Elizabeth believed he should be punished as a traitor. In this she showed him no mercy. But neither did she single him out for extraordinary punishment. Not only would this have been unjust, as she saw it (though, with the willing consent of Parliament, well within her rights), but it would risk making a martyr of Parry. Even more important, a unique and uniquely horrific form of punishment would make it seem as if Elizabeth were exacting a personal vengeance against Parry. Elizabeth understood what all effective leaders instinctively understand or soon learn: Whenever possible, deal with issues, not people. In conflict or in the extreme instances calling for reprimand, avoid making it personal. The message Elizabeth wished to send the people was that the crime at issue was not a threat against herself as a person but was treason against the state. She did not want to make the mistake of reducing a matter of great political consequence to a matter of a would-be murderer punished by his intended victim.

No leader was more aware of the importance of the personal touch in government than Elizabeth. An effective leader needs to come across as a human being who relates to other human being on a human level. But when conflict arises or when it is necessary to enforce some negative sanction, the most productive course is to depersonalize the process lest the action be trivialized or misinterpreted as having been motivated by personal feelings. Keep the focus on the most consequential issues at stake.

102. GIVE UP YOUR PRIVACY
On a Stage

In responding to the parliamentary petition asking her to sign Mary, Queen of Scot's death warrant, the queen replied that she wished she could save Mary Stuart, a kinswoman and a monarch, but that neither she nor Mary was a private person, and the matter had gone beyond the possibility of private forgiveness. "We Princes," Elizabeth told the parliamentary deputation that brought her the petition, "are set on stages, in the sight and view of all the world." The implication was clear: Mary had committed not merely a personal crime but a crime against the state, a crime that imperiled rightful religion and the well-being of the people.

Leaders, Elizabeth understood, give up their privacy and become, like it or not, public persons. They cannot always act in accordance with their personal inclinations but often must make difficult decisions based on what is best for those they lead. Signing the death warrant of Mary, Queen of Scots was, for Elizabeth, such a decision.

103. MAKE IT DEEP, SHARP, AND CLEAR
Drawing the Line

Elizabeth had gone to extraordinary lengths both to control and protect Mary, Queen of Scots. In 1585, however, it was discovered that one Anthony Babington, a young gentleman of Derbyshire and a familiar of the French ambassador, had written to Mary to tell her that he and five others were planning to assassinate Elizabeth while others would ride to the rescue of Mary herself, the rightful queen of England. The discovery of this plot—and Mary's quiet complicity in it—sealed the fate of the deposed queen of Scotland. Elizabeth wrote to Sir Amyas Paulet, who now had custody of Mary: "Let your wicked murderess know how with hearty sorrow her vile deserts compel these orders [of execution], and bid her from me, ask God forgiveness for her treacherous dealings toward the saviour of her life many a year, to the intolerable peril of my own, and yet not content with so many forgivenesses must fault again so to horribly far passing woman's thought."

Even now Elizabeth regretted having to order Mary's death, but the woman's betrayal left no choice. The original letter is missing, but it is believed that Elizabeth wrote to Mary herself: "You have in various ways and manners attempted to take my life and to bring my kingdom to destruction by bloodshed. It is my will that you answer the nobles and peers of the kingdom, as if I were myself present."

The line had been drawn, and Mary had crossed it. Tolerance and generosity are typically the marks of an effective leader, but these qualities must not be taken so far that they distort the basic reality that actions have consequences. A leader must set the limits of acceptable actions and permitted behavior. When these limits are transgressed, corrective action is required. Elizabeth was now resolved, as she should have been—indeed, as she *had* to be.

104. BEYOND RECONCILIATION—OR REHABILITATION
Termination

When the earl of Essex received Elizabeth's message to him, pointing out that if she had *wanted* to lose Ireland, she would not have sent him to save it (see 123, "Put It in Writing," 124, "Look Good, Act Better," and 125, "Evaluate Results, Not Promises"), the distraught commander abruptly deserted his post and rode off for England to explain his actions in person to Elizabeth. He arrived at Elizabeth's palace at Nonsuch on September 28, 1598, having ridden hard all night. It is reported that Essex burst into the queen's bedchamber, his clothing spattered with mud. Whatever explanations he offered, Elizabeth did not buy them. Results spoke louder than her former favorite could. On October 2, Elizabeth dismissed Essex from all his offices. She fired him. She wanted to take further action as well, to put him on trial in the Star Chamber, the special court devoted to crimes against the state. From this course she was dissuaded by her advisers; they warned her that Essex was too popular to put on trial and that to do so would provoke unrest among the people.

But Elizabeth did banish Essex from her court, and when a message from Essex was delivered to her, she turned on the messenger with rage in her voice: "By God's son," she exclaimed, "I am no Queen, that man is above me." If I compromise now, I also compromise my own authority. It is difficult to fire a friend. It is difficult to punish someone you like. But leadership often requires doing difficult things, and Elizabeth had always been willing to accept this truth. She accepted it even now.

As it turned out, Essex did not accept his "termination" with good grace. The fact is that, deprived of all his offices, he was broke and desperate. Feeling that he had nothing more to lose, Essex conspired in an abortive plot to overthrow Elizabeth and place Scotland's James VI on the throne in her stead. On February 7, 1601, Essex refused a summons to appear before the Privy Council. On the 8th, four court officials went to fetch him. The officials were mobbed by Essex's supporters, and the earl himself took the four hostage. He then set out with a band of two hundred armed men to incite a rebellion in London. Robert Cecil, who had replaced his late father as secretary of state, was a jump ahead of Essex, however, and sent a herald behind him and his followers to proclaim the man a traitor. After a brief skirmish, Essex returned to his house to find that his hostages had been liberated. By that evening Essex realized his rebellion was hopeless, and after burning his personal papers, he surrendered.

There was no alternative now but to try him in Star Chamber for treason. His request for a private execution was granted. When he died, on February 25, 1601, he prayed aloud for the long life of the queen.

*. . . By nature a practical woman
with a keen commercial sense
considered unusual not to say
unnatural in a woman.*

—CHRISTOPHER HIBBERT,
The Virgin Queen: Elizabeth I, Genius of the Golden Age

Nine

QUEEN OF THE BOTTOM LINE

DOING BUSINESS WITHOUT EXCUSES

E LIZABETH, *A LEADER OF GREAT SPIRITUAL FORCE AND PER-sonal magnetism, devoted a large portion of her genius to cre-ating and maintaining her popular image as the Virgin Queen, an almost supernatural presence on earth. Yet she did not rule by spirit, personality, or image alone. She was eminently practical, a hard-nosed pragmatist with an eye on the bottom line and absolutely no tolerance for waste, for excuses, or for the airy and endless arguments of theoreticians.*

105. KNOW YOUR BUSINESS
"The Queen of England, I Know Not How, Penetrates Everything"

Everyone who worked with Elizabeth—her privy councillors, courtiers, and ambassadors—agreed with the clerk of the council, Robert Beale, that she was a "princess of great wisdom, learning and experience"—qualities the more impressive because this judgment was made of her in her youth. It was not just that she was smart, as one courtier, Sir John Harrington, observed, but that she displayed great "understanding and learning." She had an extremely retentive memory and directed her attention to every significant detail. Her secretary of state, William Cecil, noted admiringly, "She was so expert in the knowledge of her realm and estate, as no counsellor she had could tell her what she knew not before."

Was this the lucky gift of genius?

Perhaps to some extent. But one thinks of Thomas Edison's famous definition of genius. "Genius," the inventor said, "is 1 percent inspiration and 99 percent perspiration."

The fact is that Elizabeth worked tirelessly at her knowledge and grasp of her "realm and estate." She demanded and devoured extensive written reports on national and international affairs. She read or had dictated to her all the workings of the Privy Council (the so-called Orders in Council), and she frequently met with individual councillors, with groups of them, and with the Privy Council as a whole. In amazement, the papal nuncio in Flanders remarked that the "Queen of England, I know not how, penetrates everything." There was, in fact, no mystery about it. She simply made it her business to learn what was going on and, equally important, what others thought about what was going on. It is significant that one of her favorite portraits of herself, painted in her home at Hatfield, portrays her in a dress that is embroidered all over with eyes and ears.

We like to think of our time as the "Information Age," but the fact is that successful leaders of enterprises great and small, in all periods of history, have always valued information above all other commodities. It is not just that being well informed creates a favorable impression on those we work with, but that thorough, timely information allows us to craft solutions to problems, to realize opportunities, and to create opportunities where none apparently exist. The effective leader is never satisfied with aged information or information gathered at second hand, but instead develops networks of reliable sources to feed him a steady stream of data. Moreover, the effective leader recognizes that his sources may have differing points of view on the information they relate, and he takes pains to acquire a precise understanding of these points of view: John in the sales department is likely to view the same set of market trends more optimistically than Jane in the production department. An effective leader goes into his job with a thorough knowledge of his business and then continuously gathers information (his eyes and ears are everywhere) that he, also continuously, weighs and evaluates, always basing his judgment on the nature of the source.

106. ACQUIRE PRACTICAL KNOWLEDGE AND TAKE REAL ACTION
A Lesson in Applied Economics

Leadership requires the intellectual ability to grasp the theoretical complexities of a situation or a problem *and* the gut-level confidence to put that theory into practical action.

The science of economics had not yet been invented during the age of Elizabeth, but men thought they knew enough to dismiss the possibility of a mere woman being able to wrap her poor mind around weighty questions of money and trade. Elizabeth proved them wrong, and she did so by applying herself to understanding the practical dimensions of an urgent, serious, and complex economic problem. An effective leader does not deal exclusively in broad principles or glib generalizations. She tackles issues directly and practically, taking the time and the effort to grapple with the details of their complexity.

When Elizabeth ascended the throne, the English currency had been seriously undermined by debasements of coinage made during the reigns of her father and her brother. That is, these monarchs had authorized the minting of coins containing a high percentage of base-metal alloy, which made them worth less than their nominal value. Early renaissance coinage was specie; it was made of metals such as gold and silver that were intrinsically valuable. During the reigns of Henry VIII and his son, Edward VI, coins came more closely to resemble currency than specie, becoming tokens of less intrinsic worth than their face value. The result, young Elizabeth recognized, was that when English merchants made purchases abroad, foreign vendors refused to accept the debased coins, and the merchants, in consequence, were forced to pay in gold. This not only impaired international trade, which Elizabeth longed to expand, but created a domestic gold shortage that soon had a disastrous effect on the rate of exchange. England was in danger of losing ground in foreign trade and of simultaneously finding itself racked by runaway inflation.

The problem wasn't new, and advisers to both Edward VI and Queen Mary had taken stabs at correcting the situation, but they had lacked the resolve to take the painful and highly complicated step of recalling the debased coinage already in circulation. In 1560, in close and intensely secretive consultation with her most trusted adviser, Secretary of State William Cecil, Elizabeth created a proclamation. It was delivered on September 27 and in effect said that all base coins in circulation were to be reduced "as nigh to their value as might be." The queen herself guaranteed that all base coins brought to the mint would be valued at the new rate and exchanged for newly minted coins of an equivalent worth.

The ambition, complexity, and imaginative scope of this undertaking in the sixteenth century is difficult for twenty-first-century people to grasp. Elizabeth aimed to pull off nothing less than a universal revaluation of her nation's money supply, to do so honestly and efficiently, and to do so without creating panic, without disrupting trade, and without triggering a calamitous crisis of economic confidence. Because there were insufficient stocks of silver at the mint to produce the required number of new coins, Elizabeth saw to it that London goldsmiths were recruited to melt down old coins and extract the pure metal from the alloy to be efficiently recycled. Through this intensive program almost £700,000 of debased coinage was returned to the mint and refined. In her proclamation, Elizabeth had pledged to share the cost of the operation with her people; in fact, the program was carried out so efficiently that the crown profited to the tune of £45,000.

Thus, according to one early seventeenth-century historian, did Elizabeth "achieve to the victory and conquest of this hideous monster of the base moneys," and the historian went on to judge this Elizabeth's "greater, yea greatest, glory." Certainly, the revaluation gave a tremendous boost to English merchants on the international market, greatly increasing their credit abroad. During Elizabeth's reign, the British economy vastly expanded, and with that expansion came a steady rise in income as well as prices. Revaluation could not halt inflation, but it did render it manageable even as it enabled English merchants to raise Britain from the status of poor cousin to the economic powers of the Continent to the wealthiest nation of renaissance Europe.

In contrast to many of today's CEOs and top-level managers, Elizabeth did not content herself with speaking in theoretical terms about a corporate turnaround. Instead, she analyzed the problem and, in concert with a trusted adviser, formulated a plan that, given sufficient resolve, could be carried out swiftly and decisively. To ensure success she vigorously followed up on all the details necessary for execution, and she provided pledges of assistance in bearing the burden of costs. She conveyed to those she led a sense of confidence, of good faith, and of practical feasibility. The consequence of such timely and committed steps was nothing less than the beginning of an economic miracle for England's fledgling international trade.

107. USE EXPERTS EXTENSIVELY
Consultants

The queen's skill with money was a source of wonder to her advisers and courtiers. For her part, she never allowed her natural talent to prevent her from consulting the chief financial experts of renaissance England, including Sir Thomas Gresham, founder of the Royal Exchange. With the help of Gresham and others, Elizabeth set about managing her estates as economically as possible, yet without alienating her tenants, and she also looked for areas in which she could reduce extravagance or eliminate waste. Indeed, it was on the topic of economizing that she most closely consulted the experts. Secretary of State William Cecil concluded that the "parsimony of her Majesty hath been a great cause of her majesty's riches."

108. REJECT CONSTRAINT
Blackmail and Deceit

In 1566, Parliament sought to force Elizabeth either to marry or to nominate a successor who would assume the throne after her death. The weapon Parliament wielded in this struggle of wills was the purse. The House of Commons refused to pass the subsidy bill—funds given to the monarch to run the government—until the queen addressed the issues of marriage and succession.

Elizabeth responded with a refusal to be "by violence constrained to do anything." Moreover, she persuaded the Parliament that the issue of marriage was her private affair and that the matter of succession had to be kept secret in order to avoid splintering the government into factions and undercutting her authority. Only the subsidy bill, Elizabeth argued, and not her marriage plans, was properly the concern of Parliament. Against this logic, Parliament yielded and passed the subsidy. In her turn, Elizabeth graciously "remitted" one-third of the subsidy—that is, she gave it back to Parliament. Instead of taking this as a sign of goodwill, however, Parliament seems to have interpreted it as a token of weakness. Emboldened, the drafters of the subsidy bill sneakily slipped into the measure's preamble the queen's promise to marry.

What the members of Parliament had not reckoned on, however, was the care with which Elizabeth scrutinized all legislation. She was a hands-on leader whose vision extended from the big picture and the broadest issues to the smallest details of government. Discovering the clause, she returned the draft legislation to Parliament with a note emblazoned across it: "I know no reason why any [of] my private answers to the realm should serve for prologue to a subsidies book. Neither yet do I understand why such audacity should be used to make, without my licence, an act of my words like lawyers' books." Again, she was reminding Parliament that their business was the subsidy, not the issue of her promise to marry, and she went on to condemn the drafters of the bill for having played a lawyer's trick in attempting to slip an offensive clause into an otherwise unrelated bill.

Leadership requires boldness, but it is true that boldness is often confused with rashness. A leader should be ever vigilant and, unfortunately, must never be *too* trusting. In dealing with the Soviets on the hazardous but vitally important subject of arms reduction and arms limitation, President Ronald Reagan was fond of quoting a traditional Russian saying: "Trust, but verify!" Elizabeth did just that, and her example remains a valuable one.

109. FOCUS HERE AND ACT NOW
"Peril Not the Present"

Through much of her reign Parliament pressured Elizabeth to marry or at least name her successor. Elizabeth, wishing to be her own mistress, resisted and successfully avoided marriage. She also wanted to avoid the perils of nominating a successor. These perils included diluting her own power and authority, creating dissension in court, creating the basis for power struggles, and creating dissatisfaction among the partisans of those she did *not* nominate. So, in 1572, when

Parliament again raised the issue of future succession, Elizabeth replied with calm reason:

> *I know I am but mortal and so therewhilst prepare myself for death, whensover it shall please God to send it. . . . My experience teacheth me to be no fonder of these vain delights [the concerns and pleasures of life] than reason would, neither further to delight in things uncertain than may seem convenient.*

The queen acknowledged her understanding of her mortality, that her life and her reign would end, and she further acknowledged that it is unwise to become too fond of the "vain delights" of mortal existence. On the other hand, it is also unreasonable to "delight in things uncertain"—that is, in things that may or may not come about: the future. "But let good heed be taken," Elizabeth concluded, "lest that reaching too far after future good you peril not the present, or begin to quarrel or fall together by the ears by dispute before it may be well decided who shall wear my Crown."

Elizabeth always acted with an eye toward long-term results, yet she never let this distant focus blind her to what lay before her eyes. She took care to not to reach so "far after future good" that she periled "the present." Accordingly, she counseled her subordinates to refrain from arguing about the future, for doing so would likewise "peril . . . the present."

A leader should not attempt to stamp out dispute, nor should she encourage carelessness or complacency about the future. Yet a leader must also encourage her subordinates to think and act in the present and to avoid creating disputes about events that have not yet occurred or possibilities that may or may not come to pass. If you try to steer your car by peering through a telescope, you will inevitably collide with the nearest object, which is quite invisible to you.

110. PUT THE HIGHEST VALUE ON TODAY
Work in the Present

Elizabeth avoided quick fixes, steps that might solve an immediate problem but create greater ones down the line. Yet she also had an uncanny ability to do what many managers, leaders, and even public figures of today call *compartmentalize*. She enabled herself to focus on the present by temporarily walling off the future. When she expressed, in a 1572 speech to Parliament, her philosophy of living and ruling in the present, she doubtless alarmed many hearers. Yet all decision makers need to cultivate something of this ability, which seemed to come so naturally to Elizabeth.

Though the queen shunned quick fixes that would create long-term problems, she also understood that a good solution available now is often preferable to a perfect solution that may come in time or not at all. Furthermore, she recognized that opportunities do not last forever but, once lost, may well be lost forever. Conversely, immediate crises, if left unattended to, typically compound, becoming more critical with each passing hour, day, or month. A leader must never sacrifice the future to the present, but neither can she sacrifice the present to the future. And if there is a contest between present circumstances and future possibilities, it is the present that must win, that must receive attention, that must be acted upon.

111. ACCOUNT FOR YOURSELF
Money Matters

Although an English renaissance monarch had considerable authority over financial matters, the power of the purse ultimately rested with Parliament. Kings and their ministers typically had to wrangle with that body to obtain the desired "subsidy" to conduct the government. On occasion, Parliament attempted to use the subsidy as a combination carrot and stick to compel Elizabeth either to wed or at least to name her successor. In these power struggles, Parliament always came out second best.

The Parliament of 1576 was more typical, however, of parliaments during Elizabeth's reign. It passed the requested subsidy immediately and without question. Sir Walter Mildmay, founder of Emmanuel College, Cambridge, and the man Elizabeth had appointed chancellor of the Exchequer (the equivalent of secretary of the Treasury) presented the bill to Parliament. He praised Elizabeth for the soundness of her fiscal policy, which had delivered the kingdom from what he called the "great and weighty" debt that had accrued during the reign of Henry VIII.

If you want to succeed in business, you must speak the language of business, which is, first and foremost, a language of dollars and all that flows from dollars—everything pertaining to risk and reward. Much can be said about Elizabeth's character, her charisma, her personal magnetism, her humanity, and the care with which she created herself in the quasi-religious image of a virgin queen. All these qualities served her well during her reign. But in addition she was a shrewd businesswoman who invested her country's money wisely, as well as her own. Even when urged to do so by advisers, she never threw cash at a problem but always analyzed it as an investment, a matter of risk versus potential reward. Although she spent large sums on her wardrobe and on jewels and the like, her entire court agreed that these were necessary to complete the picture of a great monarch. Moreover, while large, these expenditures were never reckless. Elizabeth tracked them with the zeal of a committed accountant. Her knowledge of finance and her prudent skill with money were well appreciated by Parliament, which most of the time—and ulterior motives aside—swiftly enacted all financial measures she called for.

Whatever else an effective leader must be, he must be fluent in the language of business. Behind the charisma is cash, and that must be dealt with persuasively, prudently, and skillfully.

112. FORMULATE FLEXIBLE RULES BASED ON REAL LIFE
Rule of Thumb

Elizabeth was pragmatic, preferring a wary flexibility to a hard-and-fast adherence to principle; however, where money was concerned, she formulated a few key rules of thumb, the most important of which was a ceiling of 10 percent on interest she would allow the Exchequer (treasury) to pay on loans. She held to this ceiling figure even in times of emergency, thereby preventing shortfalls and curbing inflation, which had run away during the reigns of Henry VIII, Edward VI, and Mary I. Doubtless, this rule often worked hardship on the Exchequer, but it was a good, practical builder of financial prudence and character.

113. CAPITALIZE ON OPPORTUNITY
Timing

While running the country, Elizabeth also kept her eyes open and her ears attuned to personal financial opportunity. She made a great deal of money on real estate, and she was especially skilled at befriending prospective purchasers of property at precisely the moment when they were eager to extend their holdings in order to set themselves up as country gentlemen. In this way, she always obtained top price on the sale of her various holdings.

114. NEVER BUILD FOR THE SAKE OF BUILDING
The Edifice Complex and How to Avoid It

Many leaders are driven by an ungovernable urge to build—to create new offices, remodel old offices, open new branches, and grow the enterprise whether it needs to be grown or not. Business needs building, no doubt about it, but beware building for the sake of building—building out of a misplaced need to leave a physical mark on the world as a token of your presence. Too many leaders suffer from an "edifice complex," the conviction that only by spending money on monuments to themselves—whether a whole new building or just a fancy office redo—can they establish their importance. In sharp contrast to her father, Henry VIII, Elizabeth steadfastly refused to spend money on new building. She limited her construction expenditures to necessary repairs—and, like any responsible homeowner, she always secured estimates first, personally examining each of them. When her secretary of state suggested that she add a new palace to the royal inventory, she replied that she had no need of palaces. Hadn't her father built more than enough?

115. DON'T TOLERATE WASTE OF TIME
Impatience

Elizabeth had notoriously little patience for long sermons and would deliberately use the time consumed by them to think about other matters, such as affairs of state. If the preacher seriously tried her patience, Elizabeth, polite in most other contexts, would not hesitate to interrupt. "Do not talk about that," she called out to the dean of Saint Paul's when he strayed into a tedious condemnation of the display of crucifixes and candles in private chapels. "Leave that! Leave that! It has nothing to do with your subject and the matter is threadbare."

Time is irreplaceable once lost. No leader should squander it or allow it to be squandered.

116. VALUE SENSE OVER SYLLABLES
"You Lawyers"

"You lawyers are so nice and precise in sifting and scanning every word and letter that many times you stand more upon form than matter, upon syllables than the sense of the law."

Elizabeth lived in an age of eloquence—the age of William Shakespeare, Christopher Marlowe, and Edmund Spenser—and was herself famed for her ability to construct complex and elaborate verbal edifices. Yet she always trusted deeds more than words, and when words were necessary, she always set substance far above form. For those who use language to obscure truth and to veil reality, who "stand more upon form than matter, upon syllables than sense," her criticism was unstinting. For a leader, language must come as close to action as possible.

117. VALUE PRACTICE ABOVE THEORY
Ropes of Sand

Although she was of formidable intelligence, Elizabeth instinctively distrusted theories and theoreticians. Her preference was always for the practical answer and the direct approach. In matters of religion, for example, she once remarked that the complex conjectures and arguments of theologians were "ropes of sand or sea-slime leading to the moon."

118. WILLINGLY EXPLAIN YOURSELF
"A Declaration of Causes"

For some years the Protestants of the Netherlands, a nation that was at the time a province of Spain, were struggling to gain independence from that Catholic kingdom. Not wishing to engage in open warfare with Spain, Elizabeth had resisted intervening in the crisis, but at last, in 1585, she assented to the Treaty of Nonsuch, which bound her to send an army to assist the Protestants. When she did this, the queen issued an extraordinary twenty-page pamphlet, *A Declaration of the Causes Moving the Queen of England to Give Aid to the Defence of the People Afflicted and Oppressed in the Low Countries.* She ordered it printed in English, French, and Dutch, and distributed not only in England, but on the Continent. What was extraordinary about it is that a sovereign ruler would feel obliged to justify her actions before the opinion of the world.

Elizabeth wrote of how the king of Spain had "appointed [to govern the Netherlands] foreigners and strangers of strange blood, men more exercised in war than in peaceable government." These men had "violently broken ancient laws and liberties of all the countries and in a tyrannous sort have banished, killed and destroyed without order of law within the space of a few months many of the most ancient and principal persons of the natural nobility that were most worthy of government." The queen pointed out that

We have by many friendly messages and Ambassadors by many letters and writings to the said King of Spain our brother and ally declared our compassion of this so evil and cruel usage of his natural and loyal people.

And furthermore as a good loving sister to him
and a natural good neighbour to his low countries
[the Netherlands] and people, we have often and often
again most friendly warned him that if he did not other-
wise by his wisdom and princely clemency restrain the
tyranny of his governors and cruelty of his men of war,
we feared that the people of his countries would seek
foreign protection.

Elizabeth took pains to avoid the impression that she was acting against a fellow sovereign, King Philip II, husband of her own late half-sister, Mary I. The fault, she argued, was on the part of the king's governors, not the king.

A leader should never feel obliged to apologize for an action, but she should be prepared to explain and, if necessary, even justify any action that might be subject to misinterpretation or an adverse interpretation. In such cases, communication is key. Justification is not the same as seeking permission. It is, rather, a method of generating wider support for a potentially risky or unpopular action.

119. COMMAND THE FACTS
Argue the Facts

Are you looking for a guaranteed method of winning all arguments? One way comes awfully close to ensuring that you'll prevail 100 percent of the time. It's not a new system of rhetoric or hypnotic mind control. It's not new at all, and, in fact, it's very obvious—so obvious that it is often overlooked.

It's called commanding the facts.

The surest way to win a dispute is to know the facts cold, then marshal them effectively.

Elizabeth was a formidable wielder of fact.

On December 4, 1559, barely a year into her reign, five Catholic bishops, deprived of their offices because they refused to take the Oath of Supremacy—which acknowledged Elizabeth (and not the Pope) as supreme governor of the Church of England—wrote to the queen, beseeching her not to advocate the new "schisms and heresies." The letter itself does not survive, but a version of Elizabeth's reply to it does. Let's take a look:

> *As to your entreaty for us to listen to you* [Elizabeth begins]
> *we waive it; yet do return you this our answer.*

With her very first sentence, Elizabeth put the bishops in their place. She asserted her authority over them by telling them that she would not stand still to listen to them— nevertheless, she would return an answer. She began with an accusation:

> *Our realm and subjects have been long wanderers, walk-*
> *ing astray, whilst they were under the tuition of Romish*
> *pastors, who advised them to own [acknowledge] a wolf*
> *for their head (in lieu of a careful shepherd) whose inven-*
> *tions, heresies and schisms be so numerous, that the flock*
> *of Christ have fed on poisonous shrubs for want of*
> *wholesome pastures.*

The accusation is powerful and eloquent, made vivid by strong metaphors built on the figure of the shepherd and his flock, which is the appropriate relation of priest to the faithful.

But it was when the queen took on the bishops' arguments one by one that the full power of her reply became apparent. Evidently, the bishops wrote that it was the Roman Church that had originally planted Christianity in England. Elizabeth countered these assertions this way:

And whereas you hit us and our subjects in the teeth that the
Romish Church first planted the Catholic faith within our
realm, the records and chronicles of our realm testify the con-
trary and your own Romish idolatry maketh you liars; wit-
ness the ancient monument of Gildas unto which both foreign
and domestic have gone in pilgrimage there to offer. This
author testifieth Joseph of Arimathea to be the first preacher of
the word of God within our realms. Long after that, when
Austin [St. Augustine] came from Rome, this our realm had
bishops and priests therein, as is well known to the learned of
our realm by woeful experience, how your church entered
therein by blood; they being martyrs for Christ and put to
death because they denied Rome's usurped authority.

Now Elizabeth turned to the historical record, citing the historical chronicle (the "monument") known as *De excidio et*
conquestu Britanniae (The Overthrow and Conquest of
Britain) by Gildas, a sixth-century British monk. The chronicle contains the story of the defeat of the Saxons, then goes
on to condemn the reign of corrupt Roman priests—led by
Saint Augustine ("Austin")—who came to power following
this defeat. Gildas claimed that the true Catholic faith had
been brought to England by Joseph of Arimathea, who
according to all four Gospels was a secret disciple of Jesus.
Tradition—not the Bible—holds that Joseph went to
Glastonbury, Somerset, as head of a dozen missionaries sent
directly by the apostle Saint Philip. Joseph of Arimathea
remains today the patron saint of Somerset. Thus, Elizabeth
argued, the Protestant Reformation sought to restore the

original church, as brought to England directly by a disciple of Christ himself and at the behest of an apostle. Only later was it forcibly polluted by "Austin" and the priests of Rome.

We, of course, could debate the historical truth of these "facts." That hardly matters. The point is that, in Elizabeth's day, the chronicle of Gildas was accepted as fact, and it was on this—not mere opinion—that the queen based her reply to the bishops.

Elizabeth continued by suggesting that certain of the bishops now protesting actually encouraged Henry VIII to break with Rome. She then concluded by citing the example of Saint Athanasius, who had once been excommunicated but was now venerated by Rome as a saint and his creed accepted. Elizabeth asks:

> Dare any of you say he [Saint Athanasius] is a schismatic? Surely ye be not so audacious. Therefore as ye acknowledge his creed, it shows he was no schismatic. If Athanasius withstood Rome for her then heresies, then others may safely separate themselves from your church and not be schismatics.

Having begun by citing historical facts (or what in Elizabethan times passed for facts) to refute the proposition that Rome introduced Christianity to England, Elizabeth used facts even more effectively to undercut the whole notion of just who was and who was not a "schismatic" (that is, a person who falsely and wrongly breaks with the "true" church). She cited Rome's inconsistency: Rome had once excommunicated Athanasius as a schismatic but now regarded him as a saint and accepted his creed. This proved he was not a schismatic, yet, like Henry VIII, he broke with Rome over what he deemed heresies. If Athanasius, in good faith, could break with Rome without falling into schism, why couldn't Henry VIII and others?

Having built her position on a firm foundation of fact, the queen closed with a stern admonition:

> *We give you warning that for the future we hear no more of this kind, lest you provoke us to execute those penalties enacted for the punishing of our resisters, which out of our clemency we have foreborne.*

It may require an exercise of our historical imagination to appreciate the devastating logic of Elizabeth's reply to the bishops, but the lesson is there for us if we take the trouble to learn it. The most effective weapon in any argument is fact— not authority, not pulling rank, not even dazzling eloquence, but fact. An effective leader, manager, or CEO needs to master and marshal the facts of any significant controversy if she expects to prevail in that controversy.

120. A PLACE FOR EVERYTHING...
Orderliness

The court of Queen Elizabeth became renowned for its orderliness, such as (according to one foreign visitor) was "never witnessed . . . anywhere" else in the world. The queen and her courtiers saw to it that ceremonies were performed punctually and properly, and that etiquette was never breached and in all details was correct. This does not mean that court occasions were stuffy or stiff. Far from it. Meals were eaten first, followed by dancing. It was during these festivities that Elizabeth called to her, one after the other, those who wished to speak. When the last courtier or petitioner had been heard, the queen rose, bade all good night, and then retired to her Privy Chamber. Typically, here she engaged in paperwork or important reading.

A sense of order does not require mechanical adherence to a routine, but it should promote efficiency and an atmosphere of calm control.

121. MAKE THE MOST OF THE LEAST
Leverage

In 1589, after the defeat of the Spanish Armada, Parliament recommended to Elizabeth that she make a full and open declaration of war against Spain. Urged by their parliaments, most monarchs would eagerly declare a glorious and righteous war. Elizabeth, however, chose not to. She turned from the urging of Parliament to the counsel of Sir Francis Drake, who had already exacted so much from Spain. Drake suggested continuing the strategy of hit and run, attacking Spanish shipping and supply rather than dueling with vast armies.

For Elizabeth it was all a question of leveraging resources. She had no desire to overawe Spain with a great and costly army if she could achieve the defeat of Spain by far more modest means. Some monarchs take inordinate pains to wreak maximum havoc on an enemy and to make the biggest possible noise in the world. Elizabeth was far more interested in what would today be called getting the biggest bang for the buck. In defiance of Parliament, she backed Drake's plan.

122. ALLOCATE RESOURCES WISELY
"For Another Prince's Town"

In 1596, a Spanish fleet dispatched from the Netherlands attacked Calais. Queen Elizabeth immediately ordered the earl of Essex to lead six thousand English troops to aid her ally, Henry IV of France. Whereas Elizabeth had rallied the defenders of her realm with uncompromising do-or-die rhetoric, to Essex she advised caution: "I charge you, without the mere loss of it, do in no wise peril so fair an army for another Prince's town." Do *not* sacrifice Calais, she admonished, but *do* remember that Calais is *French* and not worth the loss of an *English* army.

The idea of victory at any cost is deeply ingrained in the minds of many leaders. This is true even for people who would never be so unreasonable as to pay an exorbitant price for anything else. Yet winning in and of itself is not an ultimate good. Pyrrhus (ca. 319 B.C.–272 B.C.), ruler of the ancient realm of

Epirus in northwestern Greece, learned this the hard way when he defeated a Roman army at Heraclea in 280—but at the cost of most of his army of twenty-five thousand men. Congratulated on his achievement, it is said that he replied, "One more such victory and I shall be lost." History forever after has called triumphs bought too dear "Pyrrhic victories."

Elizabeth had no interest in achieving such a triumph. She never let the mere idea of winning tempt her into losing all. For her, each decision involved a kind of cost-benefit and risk-reward analysis. A passionate leader, she nevertheless strove to make these determinations in the cool light of reason.

123. PUT IT IN WRITING
Argument Settled

Arguments are inevitable in any enterprise involving more than a single person. Nor are arguments necessarily unproductive or counterproductive. They may even lead to solutions. What is destructive, however, is when an argument takes on a life of its own, assuming a never-ending circularity of sez-you, sez-I. Elizabeth, according to one of her courtiers, had a foolproof method of preventing arguments from becoming circular and self-sustaining. She would carefully write down what a certain adviser said, then take out the document weeks, months, or even years later when the adviser in question had changed his mind or altered or reversed course. Thus, the queen would argue the man down with his own former opinions.

She used this technique to criticize the earl of Essex who had persuaded her to send him in command of an army to put down the Irish rebellion led by Hugh O'Neill Tyrone. In lobbying for the position of commander, Essex had delivered to the queen detailed criticism of how his predecessors had handled the military situation in Ireland. Now, in response to a report Essex sent her from Ireland, Elizabeth used Essex's original criticism against his present performance.

Essex reported on a two-month campaign in which little had been accomplished. In response, Elizabeth cut to the heart of the matter: "For what can be more true . . . than that your two months' journey hath brought in never a capital rebel, against whom it had been worthy to have adventured one thousand men[?]" No important rebels had been captured despite the enormous expense of maintaining an army of sixteen thousand infantrymen and a thousand cavalry in the field. True, Elizabeth conceded, Essex had captured the castle of Cahir, but "you would have long since [that is, in the past] have scorned to have allowed it for any great matter in others to have taken an Irish hold [castle] from a rabble of rogues, with such force as you had, and with the help of cannon, which was always able in Ireland to make his passage where it pleased." In other words, you are now boasting of having accomplished what you would have earlier mocked in others: the use of a mighty military force—with artillery, no less—to take a shabby castle held not by an army but by a mere "rabble of rogues."

The argument settled, Elizabeth then put the dispute in a much larger and more important context. This was not just a matter of who is right and who was wrong; it was of far greater consequence. Essex's unproductive actions were expensive, draining funds from the queen's subjects who "groan under the burden of continual levies and impositions [taxes], which are occasioned by these late [recent] actions." Wasteful conduct of the war in Ireland was hurting the people of England.

Winning an argument is never sufficient justification for the argument. The outcome of a dispute should not end with gratification of one ego and the mortification of another. If it does not produce something greater than this, the argument is idle and perhaps even destructive. Elizabeth proved her point but then went on to explain the greater significance of her point. She not only used facts to settle an argument once and for all, but also made sure that Essex understood the true importance at the heart of the argument.

124. LOOK GOOD, ACT BETTER
"Nobility of That Kingdom"

Image without substance does not long stand. Nevertheless, no leader can long produce optimum results if his image is tarnished or compromised. While Elizabeth set more store by substance than by image, it is undeniable that she devoted great effort to creating and then maintaining an image to enhance her royal role. In the failure of Essex to capture or kill the chief Irish rebel Hugh O'Neill Tyrone, Elizabeth saw her image and that of her realm sorely threatened. She wrote to Essex that it was being said "that the Queen of England's fortune (who hath held down the greatest enemy she had) to make a base bush kern [backwoods peasant] to be accounted so famous a rebel, as to be a person against whom so many thousands of foot and horse besides the force of all the nobility of that kingdom must be thought too little to be employed." That is, people were pointing at her mockingly, saying that she who had put down the mighty Spaniards was now bested by a mere Irish peasant against whom thousands of English troops were insufficient to prevail. She was being made to look incompetent, foolish, and even powerless. And she did not like it.

When Essex replied to Elizabeth's complaint by offering a batch of excuses for why he should not attack Tyrone that year, the queen fired back:

> *Our Lord-Lieutenant we do tell you plainly, and you that are of our Council, that we wonder at your indiscretion. If you say that our army be in a list nineteen thousand, that you have them not, we answer then to you, our Treasurer, that we are evil served, and that there needs not so frequent demands of full pay. If you say that the muster-master is to blame, we must muse then why he is not punished. We say to you our General that all defects by musters have been affirmed to us to deserve to be imputed to the General.*

In other words: Either you have the men to do the job, or you do not. If you do not, then I am being lied to. If you do, why aren't you doing the job?

A leader expects accountability and does not hesitate to demand it. But accountability must be precisely defined. Elizabeth did not indulge in name-calling or subjectively based assessments. She did not call Essex an incompetent commander. Instead, she focused on numbers: Either you have the men to do the job, or you don't. I am being asked to pay for the men, so I must assume you have them. Accountability should be about verifiable facts and quantifiable performance. Anything else is a matter of opinion centered on personalities rather than issues. Such a focus never definitively settles a dispute or corrects a problem situation. The effective leader learns to restrain the natural tendency to call names and to express feelings, choosing to focus instead on what can be objectively evaluated and proved.

125. EVALUATE RESULTS, NOT PROMISES
Results

On September 7, 1598, the earl of Essex, having led seventeen thousand men at great risk and expense into Ireland, met with Hugh O'Neill Tyrone. Essex promised the rebel leader a full pardon if he agreed to submit to the queen's authority.

Considering the massive forces at his disposal and (from the English perspective) the magnitude of Tyrone's treason, it was a dumbfounding offer. When Elizabeth received word of this promise, she responded to Essex without anger but with something far more penetrating: the facts. "It appeareth," she began, "by your journal that you and the traitor spoke half an hour together without anybody's hearing, wherein though we that trust you with our kingdom are far from mistrusting you with a traitor, yet both for comeliness example and your own discharge, we marvel you would carry it no better." By assuring Essex that she did not think *him* a traitor, Elizabeth unmistakably implied that others would deem him exactly that. Why? The answer could be summed up in a single word: *results.*

"We marvel," Elizabeth continued, "you would carry it no better." This is classic—and devastating—understatement. Given seventeen thousand troops and the queen's full support, how could Essex have settled for no more than Tyrone's promise to behave in return for a full pardon? Now Elizabeth summed up the matter in a single sentence: "If we had meant that Ireland, after all the calamities in which they have wrapped it, should still have been abandoned, then it was very superfluous to have sent over a personage such as yourself." If I wanted to abandon Ireland, I would not have sent you to save it!

Essex had long been a favorite of Elizabeth, who over the years had endured from him much of what she called "impudence." Now he had gone too far, and Elizabeth would not let her personal feelings for him obscure the gravity of the results he had produced and, more important, had failed to produce. It was on these that she turned her focus.

*"All my possessions for a
moment of time."*

—*Reported as the last words of Elizabeth I, 1603*

Ten

WINNING

A GREAT LEADER ASSESSES HERSELF

WHAT REALLY AND FINALLY COUNTS IN LEADERSHIP? *What is the calculus of winning? The sum total of success? Through a reign of forty-five years, Elizabeth kept her eye on the prize.*

126. VALUE YOUR WORD AS THE "WORD OF A PRINCE"
Honor and Honesty

Honor and honesty: "She valued them both throughout her life," Elizabeth's modern biographer Maria Perry observes, "and she set a high value on telling the truth." But then Perry continues: "For her country she could be magnificently devious, complex and prevaricating, but she saw herself as

235

straightforward, plain-dealing and bound by an invisible power, higher than hers, never to go back on her word—'the word of a Prince.'"

Today, many business leaders look upon honor and honesty as excess baggage or as unaffordable luxuries—stuff that gets in the way of *real* business. In this respect, such "modern" people resemble the portrait that Elizabeth's Italian elder near-contemporary Niccolò Machiavelli painted of the ideal renaissance leader in his 1513 book, *The Prince*. The book became so famous that the adjective "Machiavellian" was soon used to describe any leader for whom morality is irrelevant and for whom any act of craft or deceit is justified in order to pursue and maintain political power. Just as many of today's businesspeople feel that this describes their reality, so, too, does it describe the political world in which Elizabeth reigned. It was a world of ruthless leaders who might not have declared as honestly as Machiavelli their abandonment of morality but who were nevertheless so skilled at bending, contorting, shaping, and torturing morality that it could become whatever they thought necessary.

Elizabeth understood this world, and as Perry implies, she was at home in it: "She could be magnificently devious, complex and prevaricating." Yet simultaneously "she set a high value on telling the truth," on "plain-dealing," on faithfulness to an "invisible power, higher than hers." How can both of these approaches to leadership be true?

Elizabeth understood and accepted the Machiavellian realities of power politics, but she always sought to harness power for the common good of her country. Machiavelli contemplated power in and of itself. Elizabeth, in contrast, saw power as an instrument, not merely to be exercised but to be applied. She could and would be devious, scheming, and obscure in order to use this instrument for the good of her country, but she needed her country always to regard her as truthful, straightforward, and plain-dealing—to accept her word as "the word of a Prince."

Generations of Americans have long been fond of quoting one of our own great leaders, Abraham Lincoln. "Honesty," he said, "is the best policy." True enough, and Elizabeth would heartily voice her agreement. But she might well have added: "It is not the *only* policy."

The leader who would emulate Elizabeth must accept honesty as the best but not the only policy. There is a higher truth, always defined in terms of what is good for the organization or people one leads, and this is not always 100 percent compatible with "plain-dealing" and being "straightforward." The best course is the honest course, but the best is not always possible. With an eye toward the common good and without destroying one's credibility, it is sometimes necessary to behave with a certain sophistication rather than straightforwardness. In any case, it will be fatal sooner or later to assume that everyone thinks of their word as the "word of a Prince." Like Elizabeth, today's effective leaders must learn to make a bargain with the Machiavellian devils, yet without selling out the core of morality and purpose founded in the common good.

127. NEVER YIELD TO THREATS
"I Will Never Be by Violence Constrained to Do Anything"

Elizabeth's unmarried state was a continual source of anxiety to many in her government, and Parliament several times attempted to pressure her into settling on a husband or, at least, defining the limits of succession—that is, who could and who could not inherit her throne. At times Elizabeth dealt with the political pressure good-naturedly. At other times, however, she responded sternly and even with indignation. In 1566, for example, she declared to Parliament that "though I be a woman yet I have as good courage answerable to my place as ever my father had. I am your anointed Queen. I will never be by violence constrained to do anything. I thank God I am endowed with such qualities that if I were turned out of the realm in my petticoat I were able to live in any place in Christendom."

Defiance is rarely a successful leadership stance, at least not in the long run. But there comes a time when authority must be defined in no uncertain terms. Pushed hard enough, Elizabeth warned that she would never yield to threats. Any effective leader must share this resolve in order to remain effective. Once one gives in to "violence"—a threat of any kind—one relinquishes authority. Furthermore, it is not a certain degree of authority that is lost but the very basis and foundation of authority. Yield to threat, and this crumbles away.

For most businesspeople the ultimate "violence" is the loss of a particular job. Elizabeth refused to be wholly identified with her job. "I thank God," she said, "I am endowed with such qualities that if I were turned out of the realm in my petticoat I were able to live in any place in Christendom." Without my position, she declared, I am still me, Elizabeth. Who I am depends on no one else. This being the case, the "ultimate" threat means little to me.

Many leaders make the mistake of confusing who they are with what they do. To the degree that you do this, you give up something of yourself; worse, you put some part of yourself under the authority of others. You become vulnerable and open to threat. Separate who you are from what you do, and you are that much less exposed to threat. You are freer, and, therefore, your authority is that much more firmly assured. Ask yourself: Who would I be without my job? The answer may give you a sense of your own strength or may warn you of your vulnerability.

128. A PRAGMATIC LEADERSHIP PHILOSOPHY
"In Being, Not in Seeming, We May Wish the Best"

To modern ears it is a cryptic utterance. The queen made it in a speech before Parliament in 1572: "In being, not in seeming, we may wish the best."

The statement is well worth some thought and deciphering, for it expresses the essence of Elizabeth's ultimately pragmatic philosophy of leadership. But before we continue, we might look first at that word "pragmatic." For many people in our day the word has taken on a negative connotation, as if it were synonymous with "unprincipled." That is, a "pragmatic" politician is one who may alter his position to suit a particular constituency, favoring slash-and-burn tax-cutting measures when speaking to Wall Street investors, say, but then pledging to safeguard and even increase Social Security funding when speaking to senior citizens. Such a connotation is unfortunate. In Elizabeth's day, "pragmatic" described anyone—but especially a political leader—who was concerned with facts or actual occurrences. This meaning is retained today as well, at least in the dictionary.

So what exactly was Elizabeth's pragmatism, her philosophy of dealing with facts and actual occurrences?

"In being, not in seeming, we may wish the best."

Plans for progress, improvement, correction, cure, and growth, the queen is saying, are meaningful only when they are applied to what actually *is* ("being"), that is, facts and actual occurrences. Applied theoretically to hypothetical situations, they have no effect; wishing the best in such situations—situations of "seeming" rather than "being"—is meaningless. It is a wish concerning something that does not exist, that has no *being* but only *seeming*.

Not only is Elizabeth explaining that she concerns herself little with hypothetical situations—and, conversely, focuses sharply on actual ones—but she also implies that her attention must be, of necessity, directed to the present. The present *is*. The future, in contrast, only *seems* to be. It has no existence.

Wishing for the best in the future is futile, useless, without effect. If we wish for the best, we must act on the present, which is all there *is,* so all that we can actually act upon. Fortunately, acting on the present does not rule out improving the future. Indeed, it is only by acting on the present reality that we can shape the future.

Elizabeth, like all great leaders, was inherently conservative in the root sense of that word: She abhorred waste. To speculate about the future, to attempt to act in the future, was, as she reasoned, impossible and, therefore, a waste of precious effort. To act on the present, on *being,* was the only effective alternative, and she seized upon it, never letting it go.

129. BEING A WOMAN OF BUSINESS
"A Mere Woman"

Today we speak of "glass ceilings" and point to the disparity between salaries paid to men versus those paid to women, and we complain of gender inequity in the workplace. Although the situation has steadily improved, it remains true that in most fields women must negotiate more obstacles than men in order to achieve the same goals.

During Elizabeth's day, however, there was no question of achieving the same goals. It was a man's world, period. "Oh, Lord!" an astonished Londoner was heard to exclaim when she first beheld Elizabeth. "The Queen is a woman!"

Elizabeth was always one to choose her battles wisely. She was no feminist, and she was not about to attempt to reorder society. Instead of arguing for her equal rights, she often took advantage of the prevailing attitude toward women and presented herself with an exaggerated mock modesty as a "mere woman" or a "weak woman." On one occasion, for example, a diplomat praised her fluency in foreign languages, to which Elizabeth replied that it was "no marvel to teach a woman to talk" but was "far harder to teach her to hold her tongue."

Such self-deprecation was typical, and it served a purpose. Elizabeth did not fear confrontation, but she did all she could to avoid it. Like a practitioner of jujitsu, she was adept at exploiting the strengths as well as the weaknesses of her opponents to achieve her own ends. If men were prepared to believe that she was a "mere woman," weaker and less intelligent than they, Elizabeth was willing to encourage this underestimation, which only made her stronger because her opponents were wholly unprepared for what her formidable intellect and will could throw at them.

130. EARN THE TRUST OF THOSE YOU LEAD
"No Greater Loss"

"My mortal foe can wish me no greater loss than England's hate. Neither should death be less welcome unto me than such a mishap betide me."

For Elizabeth the worst possible fate she could imagine was to lose the love of the English people. This is not to say that Elizabeth guided her actions in order to make herself likable. The "love" of her subjects was not a matter of being popular but of leading the nation in such a way that her subjects never lost faith in her and always believed that she had their good uppermost in mind and deepest in heart. Too many business leaders—from supervisors and managers all the way up to CEOs—believe that the sole measure of success is popularity. In fact, the *measure* of success may be simpler and shallower than this. In business, the measure of success is the bottom line, a matter of dollars. This, however, is not the *purpose* of leadership, for achieving that bottom-line measurement requires many skills as well as a commitment of character. The latter may be "measured" by how bad you would feel if you lost the respect and the confidence of those you lead. Measure your feelings against those of Elizabeth for whom death itself would not be less welcome than "England's hate."

131. SET GOALS WORTH WINNING
Keeping Score

Sometime between 1579 and 1584, Elizabeth composed a tiny book of prayer, a miniature volume measuring just two by three inches and written by hand in beautiful script. Six prayers are offered, two in English, one in Italian, another in French, one in Latin, and the final one in Greek. In one of the English prayers, the queen observes: "Thus in these last and worst days of the world when wars and sedition with grievous persecutions have vexed almost all Kings and Countries round about me, my reign hath been peaceable and my Realm a receptacle to thy afflicted church."

Leaders cannot resist keeping score, comparing their work to that of others. Most modern management gurus advise against this practice, suggesting that the leader's objective should be to deliver his personal best, which he should not gauge against anyone else. But the fact is that there is no reason to resist the impulse of comparison provided that you devote thought to just what it is you are comparing. Identify the truly important, worthwhile goals first, *then* look at yourself and others in terms of these goals.

In her prayer, Elizabeth shows a crystal clear understanding of her chief purpose as sovereign of her nation: to bring peace and stability to her people, which (as she sees it) is an achievement linked to making her nation a "receptacle" to true religion. Having identified the criteria by which she wishes to judge her work in comparison with that of others, she assesses the condition of the world. What she finds are nations and rulers in tumult, vexed with "wars," "seditions," and "grievous persecutions." And what she is able to say of herself, in contrast, is that "my reign hath been peaceable and my Realm a receptacle to thy afflicted church."

We all need milestones and markers of progress. Begin by choosing the right ones, the important ones. Only then can you assess where you *and others* stand in relation to them. In this way, keeping score becomes something more than the empty object of a hollow game.

132. MARRY POWER TO PRUDENCE
"Prudently with Power"

In one of the prayers Elizabeth composed for the miniature book written sometime between 1579 and 1584, she asked, "So teach me, I humbly beseech thee, thy word and so strengthen me with thy grace that I may feed thy people with a faithful and true heart and rule them prudently with power."

The earnest prayer is revelatory, telling us what Elizabeth, as ruler, most wanted. It was to provide for her people—to "feed" them—in a manner both faithful and true. And it was also to possess power, but to apply it prudently.

Note that the prayer is personal, a request for power, and, even more, it is a prayer on behalf of the nation, the people, the enterprise. An effective leader learns to think of her needs and faculties as inseparable from those of the people she leads. Power may be an attribute of a leader, but it is useless as such until it is *applied,* and it is worse than useless—it is destructive—if this is not done prudently. The effective leader thinks of her power not in terms of an attribute of self, but as a force to be used judiciously, toward the end of "feeding" the people: of leading them to sustenance and prosperity, of sustaining and advancing the enterprise.

133. ENDS RARELY JUSTIFY MEANS
"Dangerous to Do Evil, Even for a Good End"

In 1589, following the death of the French queen Catherine de Médicis, Henry of Navarre successfully attacked Paris and won the throne of France as Henry IV. He was a Protestant who thrice refused to convert to the Roman Catholic faith, and these noble refusals won for him the support of Elizabeth, who extended to him military and financial aid. But in July 1593, Henry, no longer able to maintain control over his own capital, Paris, suddenly converted to Catholicism, remarking offhandedly that "Paris is well worth a Mass." Elizabeth immediately dispatched a letter to him:

> *My God! Is it possible that worldly considerations can so erase the fear of God which threatens us? Can we in reason expect any good result from an act so impious? He who has supported and preserved you through the years, can you imagine that he will forsake you in time of greatest need? Ah! It is dangerous to do evil, even for a good end. I hope that you will return to your senses.*

Elizabeth was a pragmatist who often sacrificed a possible future benefit for the sake of achieving some particular good in the here and now. She was also a practitioner of practical faith, resting her confidence in God even as she saw to it that her nation was well defended, her troops thoroughly trained, and their armor in good order. Yet Elizabeth never lost an edge of idealism and a clear sense of the greater good. She had no hesitation about wielding power, nor did she scruple (for example) to officially authorize piracy against Spain. But she was no renaissance Machiavellian, a believer in the end always justifying the means. "It is dangerous," she said, "to do evil, even for a good end."

For her, in moral and ethical terms, means and ends were inseparable. Good ends achieved through evil means would forever be tainted by those means. There was no easy out. Forsake what you believe or know is right to achieve an end that appears useful, beneficial, profitable, and productive, and you give up the high ground of moral authority.

Value judgments are part and parcel of leadership. Value is never simply a matter of dollars but of what is *actually* gained at a *real* cost. As Henry IV saw it, Paris might have been worth a Mass, but as Elizabeth saw it, not even Paris was worth forsaking the ultimate good, true religion and true faith.

There is more to this story. Although Elizabeth chided Henry for having done evil for a good end, she did not spurn him. Despite his conversion, which she deplored, Elizabeth maintained the alliance with Henry, which she felt was essential to the well-being of England.

134. NEVER STOP LEARNING
Philosophy

Elizabeth never lost her love of learning. In 1593, she translated *The Consolation of Philosophy* from its original Latin into English. The author of the work was Boethius, who was born sometime between A.D. 470 and 475, probably in Rome, and who became a high official in the court of Emperor Theodoric. Sometime after 520, Boethius suddenly fell out of favor with Theodoric and was convicted of treason. In prison, under sentence of death, he wrote his masterwork, *De Consolatione Philosophiae*. In it, Boethius personifies philosophy as a woman who consoles him, the condemned Boethius, with the knowledge that, despite present and particular injustice, there exists a *summum bonum* (highest good), which ultimately governs the universe. Particular fortune and misfortune are subordinate to this highest good, this providence. Although human beings have free will, free will cannot undo the divine order or compromise God's universal foreknowledge. As for human virtue, despite all appearances, it never goes unrewarded.

Free will and virtuous action clearly intrigued Elizabeth, for she devoted extra care to translating these passages:

There lasteth also a viewer of us all the foreknowing
God whose ever present eternity of sight agreeth with
the following property of our actions and so dispenseth
to good reward, to ill their deserts. Neither in vain do
we put our trust in God, neither of small price our
prayers, which being truly made can never fall in vain.
Avoid vice therefore, prize virtue, your minds lift up
to true hopes and settle your humble prayers in
highest place.

While God foreknows all, His "ever present eternity of sight" agrees with our own actions, and He therefore rewards good acts and punishes evil acts. Prayer, truly made, is always effective, provided that it is animated by virtue, which is always to be prized.

Elizabeth's sense of morality and ethics was born in religion, but it was no knee-jerk product of the lessons of priests and the Bible. It was important to her to understand that virtue—righteous action—was a product of free will, of choice, of conscious, often difficult decision, which coincided with Divine Providence but was not passively obedient to it. That is, while right and wrong are eternal and absolute, human beings are not automatically or necessarily virtuous or right. They must still choose how they act.

Leadership, Elizabeth believed, rests on responsibility and the full acceptance of responsibility. This was the foundation of her leadership philosophy.

135. SHOULDER THE
LEADERSHIP BURDEN
"To Be a King"

In one of her great late speeches to Parliament—the so-called Golden Speech of 1601—Elizabeth observed: "To be a king and wear a crown is a thing more glorious to them that see it than it is pleasant to them that bear it."

This expressed what was for Elizabeth perhaps the ultimate lesson of her long reign. For anyone who aspires to leadership it is a sobering thought as well. Leadership has its rewards, to be sure, but its burdens are heavy and perhaps outweigh those rewards. It is best for leader and for led that this be understood and accepted from the beginning.

136. A LEADER IS JUST
"A Single Eye to Justice and Truth"

In her last speech to Parliament, on December 19, 1601, Elizabeth presented a concise review of her reign and her policies. It was as if she realized that this would be her final speech, her peroration, the summation of her career. Among her proudest claims was that she "never entered into the examination of any cause without advertisement [that is, without giving full notice], carrying ever a single eye to justice and truth. For though I were content to hear matters argued and debate pro and contra as all princes must that will understand what is right, yet I look ever as it were upon a plain tablet [a blank slate] wherein is written neither partiality nor prejudice."

A leader is just. Justice begins with what Elizabeth calls "advertisement," a calling for all sides to present their views so that all interested voices may be heard. Next, those voices must be heard without prejudice—the tablet plain, the slate clean—and the matter weighed on its merits and on its merits only.

Elizabeth presented this procedure as an absolute requirement for "all princes [who] will understand what is right." For right can never be a function of preconception.

Appendix

AN ELIZABETHAN
CHRONICLE

A TIMELINE OF THE AGE OF ELIZABETH

1509: Henry VIII, son of Henry VII, ascends the throne of England at age eighteen.

1516: Mary Tudor (the future Mary I, "Bloody Mary") is born to Henry VIII and Catherine of Aragon.

1533: Without papal permission, Henry VIII divorces Catherine of Aragon (who bore no male heir) to marry the young Anne Boleyn. Elizabeth Tudor (the future Elizabeth I) is born to Henry and Anne this year.

1534: Having defied the Pope in divorcing Catherine of Aragon to marry Anne Boleyn, Henry VIII pushes through Parliament the Act of Supremacy, breaking with Roman Catholicism to establish the Anglican Church, of which he is head. England begins the tumultuous process of becoming a Protestant country.

1535: The great scholar and humanist Sir Thomas More is executed because he cannot in conscience acknowledge Henry VIII as head of the church.

1536: Anne Boleyn having failed to bear Henry a son, the king engineers her trial for treason. Elizabeth's mother is executed on May 19; on May 20, Henry marries Jane Seymour, one of Anne's maids of honor. By act of Parliament, Elizabeth is declared a bastard.

1537: Jane Seymour gives birth to Edward Tudor (the future Edward VI), a male heir but a sickly infant. Jane dies eleven days after giving birth.

1540: Henry marries Anne of Cleves, a German Lutheran. The marriage is intended to gain England the support of continental Protestants against threats from Catholic nations, particularly Spain and France. Henry soon divorces Anne, whom he finds unattractive, and charges the arranger of the marriage, his chief adviser Thomas Cromwell, with treason; Cromwell is executed. Henry immediately marries the beautiful Catherine Howard.

1542: Henry discovers that Catherine has had lovers before marriage and believes she is currently committing adultery; either "offense" is treasonous under English law, and Catherine Howard is executed.

1543: Henry marries the last of his six wives, Catherine Parr.

1547: Henry VIII dies and is succeeded by nine-year-old, sickly Edward VI.

1547–53: The boy Edward VI reigns under the regency of powerful nobles. During this time, England becomes increasingly a Protestant country.

1549: Elizabeth is suspected of complicity in scheming against Edward's throne and is held under quasi–house arrest during the balance of her half-brother's brief reign.

1553: Edward VI dies of tuberculosis at age sixteen. Although Henry VIII had declared Mary Tudor, his daughter with Catherine of Aragon, illegitimate, his will named her second in succession after Edward. She now ascends the throne as Mary I. John Dudley, earl of Warwick and duke of Northumberland, stages an insurrection to put his daughter-in-law, Lady Jane Grey, on the throne in place of Mary. Jane Grey actually reigns for nine days before the insurrection is put down. Jane Grey and Dudley are executed.

1554: Mary I marries Philip II of Spain, son of the Holy Roman emperor Charles V. The marriage, part of Mary's program to restore England to the Roman Catholic fold, creates religious unrest and brings England to the verge of civil war. The union of Mary and Philip also embroils England in Spain's ongoing wars with France. Sir Thomas Wyatt and others organize a rebellion in Kent and march on London. The rebellion is quickly crushed and Wyatt executed. Elizabeth, falsely suspected of complicity in the Wyatt affair, is sent to the Tower of London; she fears (quite justifiably) that she will share the fate of her mother, Anne Boleyn, on the chopping block.

1555-58: Mary earns the sobriquet "Bloody Mary" because of her program of anti-Protestant persecution, during which some three hundred Protestant leaders are burned at the stake. Her brutal intolerance increases her great unpopularity with the English people.

1558: England loses Calais, its last possession on the Continent, to France. On November 17, 1558, Mary dies, childless. Elizabeth ascends the throne.

1558-68: Thanks to Elizabeth's charisma, political skill, and plain good sense, the first decade of her reign is prosperous and surprisingly serene. However, Elizabeth's persistent evasion of marriage causes great concern among the nobles, who worry about succession to the throne and establishing important foreign alliances.

1559: Parliament passes the Second Act of Supremacy, which definitively does away with Catholicism as the state religion and makes Elizabeth "supreme governor" of the Anglican Church. Gradually, the queen enforces uniformity of religious worship across England in order to stabilize the state religion and, thereby, the state itself.

1559-60: Elizabeth sends troops to Scotland to help local forces eject French troops stationed there; the move is intended to forestall a French invasion of England itself.

1560: Elizabeth masterminds the recall and revaluation of "base coinage"; it is a massive, complex, brilliant, and entirely successful economic move that stems ruinous inflation and instantly revitalizes the English economy.

1562: Elizabeth sends troops to France to aid the Huguenots (French Protestants) in their fight against persecution by Catholics.

1566: Despite her popularity, the success of her government, and the wisdom of her religious policy, Elizabeth faces a major challenge to her throne in her first cousin (once removed), Mary, Queen of Scots. A Catholic, Mary enjoys the support of disaffected Catholics in England who want her to rule in place of Elizabeth. Mary's boy-husband, Francis, died in 1560, leaving the queen a widow at the age of eighteen. In 1565, she married her cousin, Henry Stewart (Stuart), earl of Darnley, a weak, vicious, but ambitious man. In 1566, in a fit of jealousy, Darnley murders Mary's private secretary and confidant David Riccio, leading Mary to believe that her life is in danger. Some believe that at this time Mary begins an adulterous relationship with James Hepburn, fourth earl of Bothwell, and that the two conceive a plot to murder Darnley.

1567: A house on the outskirts of Edinburgh, where Darnley is recovering from an illness, suddenly explodes; Darnley is strangled as he tries to escape the conflagration. Under a cloud of suspicion, Mary, Queen of Scots is forced to abdicate to her son, James VI (the future James I, king of England). He reigns through 1625 (from 1603 as king of both England *and* Scotland).

1568: As a result of suspicion cast on her by Darnley's murder, the deposed Mary flees to England (after the defeat of her supporters in the Battle of Langside), seeking to be protected from the Protestant Scots lords who would try her for murder and treason. Elizabeth does not want to participate in the overthrow, let alone execution, of a rightfully constituted fellow sovereign, but she must also prevent Mary from acquiring a following and making a move on the throne of England.

1568–72: Hostilities with Spain escalate during this period.

1569: A group of earls rebel against Elizabeth in the north of England; the rebellion is quickly crushed.

1570: Pope Pius V excommunicates Elizabeth and effectively invites her overthrow and/or assassination.

1571: The "Ridolfi plot" calls for an invasion of England by Spanish troops stationed in the Netherlands; it is quickly discovered and crushed.

1572: The duke of Norfolk is executed for complicity in the Ridolfi plot.

1573: English-Spanish relations briefly improve with the ascendency in France of the moderate Guise family who look for conciliation with the Protestants.

1576–78: Martin Frobisher explores North American waters in the vicinity of Greenland; he is the first English seafarer in the New World.

1577: Elizabeth signs an alliance with the Republic of the Netherlands, which is in rebellion against Spain. Despite the alliance, she manages to avoid outright war with Spain.

1577–80: Sir Francis Drake, commissioned by Elizabeth as a privateer (state-sanctioned pirate), circumnavigates the globe, opens up parts of the New World to England, and conducts severely crippling (and highly profitable) raids on Spanish and Portuguese colonies and shipping.

1582–83: In the "Edinburgh Raid," partisans of Mary, Queen of Scots capture James VI and hold him prisoner for ten months.

1583: Sir Humphrey Gilbert establishes the first English colony in North America, at Newfoundland.

1584: Sir Walter Raleigh sponsors exploration of North American sites for the establishment of a British colony.

1585: James VI concludes a formal alliance with Elizabeth, thereby ending the national wars between England and Scotland.

1585–86: Drake raids Spanish possessions in the Carribean, again with great success and effect. The first English settlement in North America is established at Roanoke Island, off the coast of North Carolina; although not present with the colonists, Sir Walter Raleigh sponsors the project.

1585–87: Elizabeth openly intervenes in the Netherlands' rebellion against Spain. The commander in chief that she sends, Robert Dudley, earl of Leicester, proves inept, incompetent, and disobedient.

1587: Drake raids the Spanish port city of Cadiz. The Spanish prepare to invade England. Elizabeth oversees preparations for the defense of her realm. After both confining and protecting her since 1568, Elizabeth reluctantly orders the execution of Mary, Queen of Scots. Having temporarily withdrawn from their settlement on Roanoke Island because of Indian attacks, one hundred settlers under Governor John White return to colonize the site.

1588: The Spanish Armada is launched, is engaged by the English, and is defeated through a combination of brilliant English seamanship and Channel storms that prove disastrous to the Spanish fleet.

1590: Shakespeare's first play, *The Comedy of Errors*, is premiered. Twenty-three other Shakespeare plays are written and premiered during Elizabeth's lifetime. (Shakespeare writes and premieres another dozen plays during the reign of James I.) The disappearance of the Raleigh-sponsored Roanoke Colony is discovered; the colonists have vanished with only a single trace, the cryptic word CROATOAN carved into a tree.

1590-99: Edmund Spenser writes *The Faerie Queene*, an epic verse allegory aimed (in part) at immortalizing the reign of Elizabeth, whom the poem calls Queen Gloriana.

1594-1603: The Tyrone Rebellion is fought in Ireland. One of Elizabeth's favorites, Robert Devereux, earl of Essex, fails to put down the rebellion during 1599–1600. (The rebellion ends early in the reign of James I, who grants Tyrone a full pardon.)

1601: The earl of Essex, long one of Elizabeth's favorites, stages an uprising against his queen. It is quickly crushed, and Essex is arrested, tried for treason, and executed on February 15.

1603: Elizabeth, in vigorous health to the end, save for a painful throat ailment beginning early in the month, dies on March 24.

RECOMMENDED READING

THE SOURCES OF *ELIZABETH I, CEO*

The Elizabethan era is among the richest, most extensively studied, and most complex of British historical periods. The books below served as the primary sources of the information and quotations in Elizabeth I, CEO. *These volumes are indispensable to anyone seriously interested in Elizabeth and the Elizabethan era.*

Beckingsdale, B. W. *Elizabeth I.* London: B. T. Batsford, 1963.

Bindoff, Stanley T. *Tudor England.* Baltimore: Penguin Books, 1950.

Black, John B. *The Reign of Elizabeth, 1558–1603,* 2d ed. Oxford, UK: Clarendon Press, 1959.

Chamberlin, Frederick. *The Private Character of Queen Elizabeth.* New York: Dodd, Mead, 1922.

———. *The Sayings of Queen Elizabeth.* New York: Dodd, Mead, 1923

Creighton, Mandell. *Queen Elizabeth.* London and New York: Longmans, Green, 1966.

Elizabeth I. *The Letters of Queen Elizabeth I.* New York: Funk & Wagnalls, 1968.

Erickson, Carolly. *Bloody Mary.* Garden City, NY: Doubleday, 1978.

———. *The First Elizabeth.* New York: St. Martin's Griffin, 1983.

Fraser, Antonia. *Mary, Queen of Scots.* New York: Dell, 1969.

Haugaard, William P. *Elizabeth and the English Reformation: The Struggle for Stable Settlement of Religion.* Cambridge, UK: Cambridge University Press, 1968.

Hibbert, Christopher. *The Virgin Queen: Elizabeth I, Genius of the Golden Age.* Reading, MA: Perseus Books, 1991.

Hurstfield, Joel. *Elizabeth I and the Unity of England.* New York: Macmillan, 1960.

———. *Freedom, Corruption, and Government in Elizabethan England.* London: Jonathan Cape, 1973.

———. *The Illusion of Power in Tudor Politics.* London: Athlone Press, 1979.

Hurstfield, Joel, and Alan G. R. Smith, eds. *Elizabethan People: State and Society.* New York: St. Martin's Press, 1972.

Jenkins, Elizabeth. *Elizabeth the Great.* New York: Putnam's, 1967.

Johnson, Paul. *Elizabeth I: A Biography.* New York: Holt, Rinehart and Winston, 1974.

Levin, Carole. *The Heart and Stomach of a King: Elizabeth I and the Politics of Sex and Power.* Philadelphia: University of Pennsylvania Press, 1994.

Mackie, J. D. *The Earlier Tudors 1485–1558.* Oxford, UK: The Clarendon Press, 1952.

Morris, Christopher. *The Tudors.* New York: John Wiley, 1967.

Mumby, Frank A. *The Girlhood of Queen Elizabeth: A Narrative in Contemporary Letters.* London: Constable, 1909.

Perry, Maria. *The Word of a Prince: A Life of Elizabeth I.* Woodbridge, UK: The Boydell Press, 1990.

Read, Conyers. *Lord Burghley and Queen Elizabeth.* New York: Knopf, 1960.

———. *Mr. Secretary Cecil and Queen Elizabeth.* New York: Knopf, 1961.

Ridley, Jasper. *Elizabeth I: The Shrewdness of Virtue.* New York: Fromm International, 1989.

Rowse, A. L. *The England of Elizabeth: The Structure of Society.* London: Macmillan, 1950.

Smith, Alan G. R. *The Government of Elizabethan England.* London: Edward Arnold, 1967.

Smith, Lacey Baldwin. *Elizabeth Tudor: Portrait of a Queen.* Boston: Little, Brown, 1975.

Somerset, Anne. *Elizabeth I.* New York: St. Martin's Griffin, 1991.

Strachey, Lytton. *Elizabeth and Essex: A Tragic History,* reprint ed. Orlando, FL: Harcourt Brace, 1996.

Strong, Roy, and Juila Trevelyan Oman. *Elizabeth R.* London: Secker & Warburg, 1971.

Thomas, Jane Resh. *Behind the Mask: The Life of Queen Elizabeth I.* New York: Clarion Books, 1998.

Weir, Alison. *The Life of Elizabeth I.* New York: Ballantine, 1999.

Wernham, R. B. *The Making of Elizabethan Foreign Policy, 1558–1603.* Berkeley: University of California Press, 1980.

Williams, Neville. *All the Queen's Men: Elizabeth I and Her Courtiers.* New York: Macmillan, 1972.

Williams, Penry. *The Tudor Regime.* Oxford, UK: The Clarendon Press, 1979.

Wilson, Charles Henry. *Queen Elizabeth and the Revolt of the Netherlands.* Berkeley: University of California Press, 1970.

Wright, Thomas. *Queen Elizabeth and Her Times.* 2 vols. London: Henry Colburn, 1838.

⇥INDEX⇤